About the author

Dr Vivien Stern is Senior Research Fellow at the School
of Law, Kings College London and Honorary Secretary
General of Penal Reform International. Her most widely
read previous book is *A Sin Against the Future:
Imprisonment in the World* (Penguin Books, 1998).

Praise for this book

'In *Creating Criminals*, Vivien Stern gives us a stunning, revealing and deeply troubling account of the growing resort to imprisonment as the default solution to the escalating social problems of a global market society. This is essential reading for anyone who cares about the future of justice – in Europe, North America, and throughout the world.' – Elliot Currie, Legal Studies Program, University of California, Berkeley

'This book sparkles with hopeful ideas about how we could reduce crime and the prison population. It shows how the worldwide move to privately owned prisons and the ideas that flow from marketed services are leading to increased fear of crime, costly prisons and cruel regimes. It outlines very clearly how we could do better.' – Clare Short, MP

'This important new book encourages the development of more humane and effective ways of preventing crime.' – Yuichi Kaido, lawyer, Secretary General of Center for Prisoner's Rights, Japan

Creating Criminals
Prisons and People in a Market Society

Vivien Stern

Fernwood Publishing Ltd
Halifax, Nova Scotia

Books for Change
Bangalore

SIRD
Kuala Lumpur

David Philip
Cape Town

Zed Books
London & New York

Creating Criminals was first published in 2006 by

In Canada: Fernwood Publishing Ltd,
8422 St Margaret's Bay Road (Hwy 3) Site 2A, Box 5,
Black Point, Nova Scotia, BOJ IBO

In India: Books for Change,
139 Richmond Road, Bangalore 560 025

In Malaysia: Strategic Information Research Development (SIRD),
No. 11/4E, Petaling Jaya, 46200 Selangor

In Southern Africa: David Philip (an imprint of New Africa Books),
99 Garfield Road, Claremont 7700, South Africa

In the rest of the world: Zed Books Ltd, 7 Cynthia Street, London NI 9JF, UK,
and Room 400, 175 Fifth Avenue, New York, NY 10010, USA
www.zedbooks.co.uk

Designed and typeset in Monotype Bembo by Long House, Cumbria, UK
Cover designed by Andrew Corbett
Printed and bound in Malta by Gutenberg Ltd

Distributed in the USA exclusively by Palgrave Macmillan, a division of
St Martin's Press, LLC, 175 Fifth Avenue, New York, NY10010

A catalogue record for this book is available from the British Library
Library of Congress Cataloging-in-Publication Data available

Library and Archives Canada Cataloguing in Publication
Stern, Vivien
    Creating criminals : prisons and people in a market
society / Vivien Stern.
    Includes index.
    Co-published by Zed Books.
ISBN 1-55266-193-8
    1. Crime--Sociological aspects. 2. Crime--Economic aspects.
    I. Title.
HV6171.S74 2006   364   C2005-907267-9

ISBN 1 55266 193 8 (Canada)

ISBN 983 2535 816 (SIRD)

ISBN 1 84277 538 3 Hb (Zed Books)
ISBN 1 84277 539 1 Pb (Zed Books)
ISBN 978 1 84277 538 7 Hb (Zed Books)
ISBN 978 1 84277 539 4 Pb (Zed Books)

Contents

Tables

In memory of Ahmed Othmani, former political prisoner, penal reformer and human rights activist, founder member of Penal Reform International and elected its Chairperson in 1994, who was killed in a road accident in Rabat, Morocco, on 7 December 2004

Foreword and Acknowledgements

This book will be hard for librarians to categorize. It is not criminology, though it draws on the thoughts of some outstanding criminologists. It is not sociology, though crime and justice policies have their roots deep in societies. Law is the basis of a criminal justice system but this is not a law book. In the end it is about politics, the politics of punishment. I hope it will be useful to readers in both the North and the South, the West and the East, and particularly to non-specialists, who can see that their system is wrong but have not had time to find out why it is wrong, what is behind the wrong and what can be done to put it right.

I owe a great deal to many people who have inspired this book and helped me to turn the idea into reality.

I have learnt a great deal from Nils Christie, whose analysis of trends in criminal justice has informed and inspired all those throughout the world who care about prisons and prisoners. Paul Farmer's work on the global injustice of health provision has thrown much light on similar injustices in crime policy and the use of prison. Many have worked to point out why a market in imprisonment poses dangers, and amongst these Stephen Nathan's dedication in collecting and disseminating information on the private prison business is unparalleled.

This book would never have reached the publishers without the assistance of Helen Fair, Research Associate at the International Centre for Prison Studies. She is speedy, accurate, resourceful, good-humoured and very skilful. I am also grateful to Rob Allen, Anton Shelupanov and Andrew Edwards of the International Centre for Prison Studies for their support.

I am grateful to Rani Shankardass, Vice-Chair of Penal Reform International, to Paul English, its Executive Director, and to all who work there, for their efforts to reform penal systems round the world and the information about that work which they have shared with me.

Robert Molteno, until recently Managing Editor at Zed Books, the initiator of the project, has been patient, supportive, unendingly helpful, wise and generous in his comments. It has been a pleasure working with him.

Finally I would like to thank Andrew Coyle, a source of inspiration and also of unfailing practical help.

Introduction

Crime and Justice in the Twenty-first Century

In 2004 a scandal was discovered in Meru prison in central Kenya. Five prisoners were found dead in a cell the size of a single bed. Seven other prisoners were also in the cell. At first it was thought that the dead men had suffocated but a post-mortem showed that they had been beaten to death. Reports said that they refused to enter the cell because it was overcrowded, so the prison guards beat them up. The cell measured one by two metres. When they got into it they were attacked by the prisoners already in there. It was alleged that when the investigation started the prison staff tried to stop the chief government pathologist from conducting autopsies. The dead prisoners were not dangerous criminals. Three of them were being held whilst awaiting trial after being accused of illegally brewing alcohol. The two others were serving sentences of just three months.[1]

In Japan in 2004 a radical plan was unveiled by the Minister of Justice. For the first time the country was to have a private prison to help cope with the rapid rise in the number of Japanese prisoners and the overcrowding in existing prisons. For many years Japan had managed with a very small prison population. But in the mid-1990s suddenly the number of prisoners began to grow. In 1995 Japan had 46,622 prisoners and an imprisonment rate of 37 per 100,000, one of the lowest in the world. By 2001 the figure was one-third higher. Private prisons were in the news. And the Japanese government was persuaded that a private prison was the solution to their over-crowding problem.[2]

In February 2003 in Bam Lam in Thailand a 42-year-old woman called Somjit Kuanyuyen was shot dead in front of her house. She had discovered three days before that she was on a police blacklist of all those suspected of having something to do with illegal drugs.[3] These blacklists appeared in January 2003 after the Prime Minister of Thailand, Thaksin Shinawatra, announced a new war, a war against drug dealers. He said, 'There is nothing under the sun which the Thai police cannot do.... It may be necessary to have casual-ties....'[4] When she heard she was on the list Somjit Kuanyuyen reported to the Bam Lam district police station. She could neither read nor write, but she put her mark on a document. Apparently she did not know what she was signing but she was reportedly told by the police that she was now safe. On 20 February four unidenti-fied men in a pick-up truck with darkened windows drove up to her house and shot her seven times in front of her seven-year-old granddaughter and her seven-months-pregnant daughter. Her house was only 20 metres from a police box but the police took a long time arriving at the scene of the crime and they did not collect the spent bullet shells. By 15 April, according to the police, 2,245 people had been killed in the 'war on drugs' announced by the Prime Minister.[5]

In the US Presidential election in November 2004 about five million people, that is roughly 2.3 per cent of the number of people eligible to vote, were prohibited by law from participating. They were disenfranchised because they had been convicted of a crime. These five million people were not a representative sample of the American electorate. They were overwhelmingly poor, and over-whelmingly African or Hispanic Americans.[6] How they would have voted if they had not lost the right and what the effects of their votes would have been will never be known.

In England in 2004 a fifteen-year-old boy called Jason had his face on a leaflet that was put through the door of every house in the housing area where he lived. The leaflets were also distributed in the local supermarket. This happened because Jason was the subject of an Anti-Social Behaviour Order (ASBO). This is a court order that is made after an application by the municipal authorities. Jason had been accused of riding a motor-bike around the housing area. The court order said that Jason could not go anywhere near the local shops. If he did he would be committing a crime and then the court could send him to prison.[7] According to a newspaper report, 'neighbours have taken to abusing him in the street and taunting him that he will soon be in prison. One woman in particular follows Jason with a camera, hoping to gather evidence that he has breached his [order] to pass on to the police.' And it was not just prison that faced fifteen-year-old Jason. If he breached his order his family could be thrown out of the house they lived in, which was rented from the municipal authorities. His mother knew Jason was a problem. She had been fighting for years to get help for his educational and emotional problems. The help did not come.[8]

These recent incidents taken from round the world all tell us something about crime and punishment in the first decade of the twenty-first century. They are very specific to their place, whether it is Meru in Kenya, an English neighbourhood, Japan, Bam Lam in Thailand or the United States of America. They reflect the policies, practices and problems of nation states. The methods of dealing with crime and the punishments for it are domestic issues under the control of national governments, and crime rates in each country are related to domestic policy. States decide for themselves what is against the criminal law, how people should be punished for breaking the law, and whether they want their prison population to go up or down.

However, crime and punishment policies are no longer insulated from outside pressures. Many aspects of life in the twenty-first century, including crime and punishment, are now subject to globalizing influences. Practices in nation states reflect patterns of policy change that come from beyond the borders of the nation state. Levels of crime are affected by the way the world economy is structured. In responding to crime in their communities governments react to worldwide pressures. The leaflets that went through the doors in the public housing project where Jason lives represent the influence of wider forces than just angry neighbours.

These influences and their consequences are the subject of this volume, the first of the Global Issues series to deal with crime and punishment. In one sense the answer to the question, 'Is there some connection between crime and forces operating around the globe?' is simple. Crime and globalizing trends are obviously interrelated because economic globalization gives many opportunities for crime on a bigger scale than was previously possible. Frauds such as those associated with big companies (Enron, WorldCom or Parmalat), where profits were exaggerated, the companies got into considerable difficulties, the people at the top enriched themselves and thousands of ordinary workers lost their pensions, are a result of the dismantling of regulation and financial controls. These relationships and developments have been well documented.[9] Criminal syndicates can use the Internet to streamline their operations, as do other multinational operators. When markets are opened up to legitimate trade they are also opened up to people traffickers or arms traders.

World-scale financial crime or cross-border crime, however, are not the subject of this book. Nor is it about crimes against humanity such as the genocide in Rwanda in 1994 and the ethnic cleansing in the former Yugoslavia. These are crimes so out of the ordinary, so huge in their impact and beyond the capacity of a single country to confront and cope with alone, that they are dealt with by the country concerned alongside international machinery set up by the United Nations. Both of these subjects have been well covered by many distinguished commentators.

This book is about crime at a much more mundane level: the crimes of the village and the neighbourhood, of towns and cities where people live and work. It is about crimes committed by ordinary people in their own countries against their own families, neighbours and those in their social circle, crimes that have no international significance at all. It is also about what acts are seen as crimes, how such crimes are dealt with, who gets punished, what punishments are used and what the consequences are.

Huge financial frauds or large-scale crimes against humanity are clearly global issues. Can ordinary crime and the way it is dealt with also be a global issue? This book will argue that it has become one because pressures from the neoliberal economic consensus are having a profound effect. They are affecting how much crime is committed. They are influencing how crime is defined. They are creating an orthodoxy about how crime ought to be dealt with by society. Also, and not surprisingly, a market in protection from crime and in dealing with convicted people is being developed that is having an effect on policy and practice worldwide.

These trends are complex and many scholars have analysed them.[10] The analysis suggests the following pattern of events. First, changes in the global economy have an effect on levels of crime. Worldwide research shows that crime levels are low when communities, built on strong family relationships, are cohesive and mutually supportive. When people's lives are based on shared values of how life should be lived and children are socialized into those values, then social norms are more likely to be accepted and followed. When communities are under great pressure – when whole industries close down, for example, as did the coal mines in the North of England or the motor industry in Detroit, and stable livelihoods are taken away – crime increases. When all members of a family, including the grandparents, have to work to keep the family afloat, children are more likely to get their values elsewhere. They learn that committing crime is the way to be respected by the group on the street. In a market society, in which the jobs go to the places where wages are cheapest and communities are left with no help and no alternatives, crime and insecurity in those neighbourhoods will rise.

Harsher attitudes to poor people and the withdrawal of social safety nets also lead to more crimes. Social order is no longer assured by socially inclusive welfare policies. Instead, policies aimed at maintaining social order concentrate on law enforcement and punishment. People do not get the support they need from state institutions to deal with social and health problems in their families. Spending on preventive action is reduced and the state action when it comes is punitive rather than supportive. The bigger the gap between rich and poor, the greater will be the levels of violence and serious crime.

In these circumstances, more acts are treated as crimes. Some acts are universally seen as crimes. Murder, rape, robbery, embezzlement and arson are seen as crimes in the laws of all countries. However, other actions can become crimes only when governments so decide. In many countries pressure from the United States and the United Nations Drug Control Programme forces governments to introduce new drug crimes, making possession of or dealing in certain substances a criminal offence. Such laws bear more heavily on some people than on others, because the major drug traffickers have money to spend on bribes and thus they can evade the criminal process. Small traffickers and users do not and cannot.

Politicians have less control over what happens in their economies. To show that they have control over some aspects of the lives of their people they turn their attention to crime. First they stoke up fear of crime and encourage demands for retribution. Then they offer their frightened populace harsher measures against the crimes of the small criminals, the poor and the least powerful. Since harsher measures are ineffective in reducing crime or the fear of crime, the results are not impressive. So the politicians promise more and then even more toughness: another few years are added to prison sentences and new crimes are created. In 2003, for example, under a new law passed in Texas, it became a crime punishable with up to ten years' imprisonment to give a prisoner a cell phone, tobacco or cash.[11] In England in 2004 it became a crime punishable with a fine of £80 (US$160) for a person under the age of eighteen to carry a firework in a public place.[12]

Global Trends

This pattern can be seen in many countries. Punishments for crimes are becoming harsher. Prison populations have risen more than 50 per cent in the last twelve years in 50 major countries, with some countries showing dramatic increases. The prison populations in Brazil and Thailand, to take but two examples, have more than doubled during those years.

Along with this shift from welfare policies to punishment policies, in many countries market forces have secured a large-scale entry into the business of crime control. The increase in crime, insecurity and levels of punishment has provided opportunities for many sorts of companies: some providing security guards, some building and managing prisons, and others selling equipment such as CCTV cameras or machines that screen people for traces of illegal drugs.

The growth in income inequality within many societies that has characterized the last two decades is also reflected in crime and policies to deal with it. Across the world it is the disadvantaged who have felt the greatest impact of these changes. They suffer most from the increase in crime. Their neighbourhoods are less likely to be protected. The rich can withdraw and live in a self-contained gated community or hire a security guard for their homes. The poor cannot. The poor are more likely to be detained by the police than protected by them, more likely to be punished by prison than by a fine or an alternative sentence, more likely to be prosecuted for drug taking. The crimes of the poor are perceived as more threatening than the crimes of the wealthy or crimes against the poor.

This is the direction being taken by many countries. Yet it can be resisted and many countries are doing so. Some governments would still rather spend money on prevention and social cohesion than on repression. Non-governmental organizations are very active, fighting against bad prison conditions and further criminalization of the poor. Many of those who work in the system as prison guards, judges, prison doctors, social workers or local mayors are holding back the moves towards more punishment and less social welfare and healthcare.

The Structure of This Book

This book contains an analysis of these trends and attempts to explain them. It starts in prison because prison is the place where the impact of these developments is very clearly seen and measured. Chapter 1 gives a snapshot of imprisonment in the world. The next chapter looks at how people end up in prison, at the connection between prison and crime, and at the ways crime is defined and recorded. 'Does prison work?' is also a question addressed in Chapter 2. Chapter 3 looks at the marketization of crime and punishment and points to the dangers that a market in punishment can bring. In Chapter 4 some light is shed on the specific impact on crime and punishment of the 'war on drugs' and the hostility to immigration from the poor world to the rich world. Chapter 5 looks at the work being done by many people across the world to resist these trends and develop policies that are just and effective.

The book ends with a suggestion for a new agenda which combines measures for safety, human security, and protection from crime with social justice. It calls for all those who want to live in a more just world in the future to find out more about how crime is dealt with in their country, who is being imprisoned, which parts of the justice system are up for sale and what they can do to change the direction of crime policies in their own society and in the wider world.

This book is not written for specialists in crime and justice. Many excellent texts are already available and are listed in the bibliography. It is designed for well-informed non-specialists, concerned about the direction of the world, growing inequality and insecurity, the use of fear in politics and the marketization of all areas of public life.

Notes

1 'Kenyan prisoners die in tiny cell', BBC News, 28 September and 'Kenyan prison bosses suspended', BBC News, 4 October 2004.
2 Hiroshi Matsubara, 'Plan for Privately Funded Prison Unveiled', *Japan Times*, 28 January 2004.
3 See Amnesty International, *Thailand: Grave Developments – Killings and Other Abuses*, 2003.
4 See Human Rights Watch, *Timeline of Thailand's 'War on Drugs'*, 7 July 2004.
5 See Amnesty International, *Thailand: Grave Developments*.
6 Brent Staples, 'How Denying the Vote to Ex-Offenders Undermines Democracy', *New York Times*, 17 September 2004.
7 Technically, in England a fifteen-year-old boy would not be sent to a prison as such, but to an institution that has another name but resembles a prison in all important respects.
8 Peter Stanford, 'Out of Order', *The Independent*, 29 August 2004.
9 See, for example, Joseph Stiglitz, *The Roaring Nineties: Seeds of Destruction*, London: Allen Lane, 2003.
10 See Suggested Further Reading on p. 200.
11 *Corrections Journal*, PaceCom Incorporated, 24 November 2003.
12 'Firework Scheme Targets under 18s', BBC News, 21 September 2004.

1

Behind the Bars:
the Injustice of Prison

Glendairy on Fire (March, 2005)

Who would have thought that on March 29th, 2005 the prisoners at the Glendairy Prison in Station Hill, St Michael, would have set fire to the island's lone adult correctional institution? For days the fire at this 150 year old penal institution made headlines not only in Barbados but across the region. While many Barbadians never saw it coming many others are of the opinion that rioting at the prison was inevitable especially since this institution which was built to hold only 300 was holding up to 997 inmates at the time. The incident allegedly occurred following a homosexual act. The interesting thing is that for a long time now several calls have been made to do something about the perturbing situation of homosexuality in the prison including suggestions to put condoms in the prison. Although the details about how and why the fire was set remain obscure at this point in time, one thing remains evident; the prisoners were discontented with their surroundings.

… Although not completely demolished, it seems that the 150 year old Glendairy Prison is no longer going to be used as a prison. Hopefully they will turn it into a museum or keep it as a historic landmark.[1]

A Bad Day in Quito Prison

Crime, justice and punishment are always in the news. They are hot topics in most countries, usually in the form of an outcry about rising crime, fear and insecurity, the resulting need for more police powers and a call for harsher punishments. At the same time the prisons of the world get fuller, infectious diseases spread within them, judges pass more severe sentences and technology is increasingly called into service to provide surveillance of convicted people. Rich countries spend more money each year on crime control and detection. Poor countries try to run complex, Western-style criminal justice systems without the requisite resources.

In this chapter we look at penal justice in the twenty-first century, as expressed by sending people to prison. Prison is the backstop of the whole process. People are held in prison after they have been arrested and before they have been convicted of a crime. Prison is the destination for convicted people who are being punished or locked up to protect society from further crimes they might carry out. Prison is the place where countries that still use the death penalty hold condemned prisoners, in a grim block called Death Row, to await the announcement of the date for their execution or to live for years whilst they submit appeals to higher courts. Every country in the world has or uses prisons.

The prisons of the world are often in the news, and rarely because the news is good. For example, an event took place in Ecuador in February 2004 that would have caused no surprise in Latin America because such things happen regularly in that region. In a prison in the capital, Quito, on a Sunday, which is family visiting day, prisoners took more than 300 of the visitors hostage. The prisoners took this action to protest at overcrowding and poor conditions.[2] The 33 prisons in Ecuador were built to house 6,000 prisoners, but actually held 12,600 at that time.[3] The prisoners were also protesting at the slowness of the judicial system. More than one thousand of them, not yet found guilty of any crime, had been in prison for over a year waiting for their trial to start.

The government began negotiations with the prisoners. They promised to release those who had waited more than a year for their trial and to build three new prisons to ease the overcrowding.[4] But their promises were not believed. The action spread and in March a similar hostage taking took place at the women's prison. Journalists were among the hostages. The situation was complicated further when the prison guards added their protest by going on strike for better pay and improved working conditions.[5] The affair ended when the police stormed the prisons and restored order. Some prisoners escaped in the turmoil. The Ecuadorian Interior Minister Raul Baca said, 'I don't know how many [inmates] have fled or were killed or wounded. We won't know this until the operation is over.'[6]

The story of the Quito prison illustrates many of the problems of prison systems around the world. Most prisoners, men and women, live in bad, unhealthy and overcrowded conditions. Prison guards suffer the same poor working conditions and are badly paid and inadequately trained. Many of the prisons of the world are always overcrowded. Disturbances are frequent and often put down with lethal force. Violent death is an ever-present possibility in the prisons of many countries. Security can be very tight but sometimes prisoners manage to escape. Governments often struggle to run humane prison systems but have insufficient resources to do so.

Improvements are promised but rarely materialize. They were not very successful in Ecuador. In June 2005 hundreds of prisoners again protested. One man was nailed to a wooden cross by other prisoners and two women sewed their lips shut to illustrate their support for a prison hunger strike. Other women cut themselves and used their blood to write placards calling for reforms. Their main demands were for electricity, running water and early release for good behaviour.[7]

Prisons and the Rule of Law

In this chapter we look in some detail at the injustice of prison. This is not to overlook the acts committed by those who end up in prison, nor the plight of those whom they have harmed. The next chapter will focus on crime, and the effectiveness of imprisonment as a response to it. Prisons are meant to be part of a justice system and what happens in them should affirm and strengthen justice, not deny it. Albie Sachs spent some time in prison in South Africa for opposing the apartheid system. When he was in exile in Mozambique in 1988 he opened a letter bomb addressed to him and lost an eye and a hand. South Africa became democratic in 1994 and he was appointed by the South African President, Nelson Mandela, as a judge in the country's first Constitutional Court. When asked to rule on the question of whether prisoners should be able to vote, Judge Sachs said:

> [p]risoners are entitled to all their personal rights and personal dignity not temporarily taken away by law, or necessarily inconsistent with the circumstances in which they have been placed. Of course, the inroads which incarceration necessarily makes upon prisoners' personal rights and their liberties are very considerable. Nevertheless, there is substantial residue of basic rights which they may not be denied; and if they are denied them, they are entitled to legal redress.[8]

Judge Louise Arbour was a member of the Supreme Court of Canada. In February 2004 she became the High Commissioner for Human Rights for the United Nations. She had a similar view to that of Judge Sachs. While she was a judge in the Toronto Appeal Court she carried out an investigation into an event at the Federal Women's prison in Kingston, Ontario. The event involved an emergency response team consisting entirely of men going into the prison after an incident, stripping a group of women naked, placing them in restraints and moving them from their cells. In the conclusions to her investigation she said that 'the legal order must serve as both the justification and the code of conduct for correctional authorities'.[9] In other words, prisons must be run according to the law and that is the only basis on which it is acceptable to take away people's liberty.

Too Many Prisoners: Not Enough Space

For most prisoners around the world the experience of prison will not be like the experience of prisoners in Denmark or Sweden, who are likely to spend their days in a workshop or education room and their nights in a single cell like a small hotel room with a radio, television and sanitary facilities. Most prison systems of the world are overcrowded, so prisoners will be living very close to each other and struggling for access to space and the basics of life.

The US State Department reported in 2003 that Luanda prison in Angola, built for 800, held 1,750 prisoners. Warehouses in Bengo, Malange and Lunda Norte provinces were used as prisons during the year.[10] In 2004 a Bangladesh newspaper reported that the oldest prison in Bangladesh, Dhaka Central, built to hold 2,650, was holding over 11,000 people, including 250 women.[11] The US federal prison system is 40 per cent overcrowded.[12] The Council of Europe, an intergovernmental human rights body with 46 member countries stretching from Lisbon to Vladivostok, has an official committee which visits places where people are detained and reports on what it finds. In 2001, in Oporto prison in Portugal, this committee, called the European Committee for the Prevention of Torture and Inhuman or Degrading Treatment or Punishment, found cells of seven square metres built for one person but holding three people.[13]

Overcrowding can be dramatic with, at the extreme, prisoners with no room to lie down pressed up against the window bars and tying themselves to them so that they sleep standing up.[14] It can mean sleeping in shifts because there are more prisoners than beds.[15]

It can mean that the weaker prisoners never get a bed to lie on, or are assigned a small space right by the cell toilet. Sometimes they are even struggling for enough air to breathe. In Russia in the mid-1990s the head of the prison service told a parliamentary committee that sometimes prisoners died in Russian prisons of suffocation because of a shortage of air.[16]

Even in rich countries prison overcrowding leads to treating prisoners as commodities rather than people. One of the directors of a prison in Vermont, USA, asked investigators looking into the deaths of seven prisoners within two years, 'Do you think I know who they [the prisoners] are, let alone [am able to] tell you that I provide them correctional and rehabilitative services? I stash them

Table 1.1

Occupancy levels in some prison systems by percentage where 100 per cent is full occupancy

Kenya	344
Barbados	302
Tanzania	191
Brazil	183
Dominican Republic	175
El Salvador	166
South Africa	164
Thailand	152
India	137
Chile	134
Bahamas	129
Mexico	126
France	118
England & Wales	110
United States of America	109
Australia	106

Source: These statistics were taken from *World Prison Brief Online* <www.prisonstudies.org>, 14 June 2005. Statistics are not necessarily from the same year but represent the most recent figures available. Percentages have been rounded to the nearest whole number.

until they are moved.'[17] The Director-General of the Prison Service in England and Wales said that with overcrowding:

> We are greatly at risk of individuals in the prison being completely dehumanised – it's a very big machine that is churning away – as individuals, they are not very important to it and they feel the weight of imprisonment at that point and it looks like a very scary world they are entering....[18]

In several prisons in Scotland the prisoners share a small cell with one other person and have to use a chamberpot in the cell because there are no better sanitary arrangements.[19]

Official figures that measure overcrowding in prisons reflect each country's own decision as to when the amount of space is not enough. There is no world standard for enough space. How much is enough will depend on how many people are in the cell, how many hours they spend in it, how much time they have in the fresh air, how much natural light and air enters the cells. The European Committee for the Prevention of Torture has suggested an absolute minimum of four square metres per person for countries struggling to reform their systems and reach minimum standards.[20] But even though countries can define overcrowding for themselves and do not have to conform to an international standard, they admit to perilous levels.

The effects of overcrowding are severe. At the worst, prisoners can contract a deadly disease or suffer lethal violence. At best, life is lived under great pressure and a struggle for access to resources. Often governments try to deal with prison overcrowding by building more prisons at great expense. Somehow prison building never manages to keep up with the growth in the number of prisoners and a few months after the new prisons are opened they are overcrowded again. The prisons of England and Wales have been overcrowded every year for the last 20 years.[21] Yet in the ten years 1992–2002, 20 new prisons were opened.[22] Levels of over-crowding fall when the new prisons open. Then, after a few

Table 1. 2
**Some countries where the percentage of pre-trial
detainees/remand prisoners is above 50 per cent**

Paraguay	92.7
Haiti	83.5
Dominican Republic	79.8
Honduras	78.6
Bolivia	77.1
Mozambique	72.9
Uruguay	72.5
India	70.4
Ecuador	69.9
Peru	69.8
Mali	67.2
Pakistan	66.1
Saudi Arabia	65.8
Uganda	65.7

Source: These statistics were taken from *World Prison Brief Online*, 14 June 2005. Statistics are not necessarily from the same year but represent the most recent figures available. Percentages have been rounded to the nearest whole number.

months, overcrowding starts again and is soon back to the level it was at before the new prisons were built.

Waiting for Trial

The prisoners in Ecuador protested because some had waited more than a year for their case to come to trial. In some countries a year would be regarded as a short time to wait. Many prisoners wait years for their case to come before a judge, some spending longer in prison than they would serve if they had been sentenced for their crime.

In all countries some of those in prison will be waiting for their trial. There are countries, however, where the majority of the prisoners locked up in prison are in that situation.

Prisons and Violence

Brazil – a bleak history

1992	111 inmates die after police storm Carandiru prison in São Paulo
2001	In a simultaneous state-wide rebellion, prisoners revolt at 29 different facilities
2002	10 people die and 60 prisoners escape during violence at the Embu das Artes jail in São Paulo
2003	84 prisoners tunnel their way out of Silvio Porto prison in Paraiba, in the biggest breakout in Brazil's history
April 2004	14 inmates are killed, some mutilated, during an uprising at Urso Branco prison in Rondonia
June 2004	An uprising at Benfica facility in Rio de Janeiro leaves at least 34 inmates dead.[23]

Prison is the place where those who break the law are sent, ostensibly to be reformed, but prisons are places that contain great contradictions. One such contradiction is that prison is part of the justice system of any country but, as the above extract about Brazil shows, prisons are often themselves places of great lawlessness, where many crimes are committed within the walls and there is no access to justice for those thus harmed. The violence in Brazil continued. In June 2005 there was a riot at a prison in São Paulo State and five prisoners were decapitated. Two prisoners were shot by military police in a prison in Recife and a prisoner was decapitated in a riot at a detention centre in Juiz de Fora in the state of Minas Gerais.[24]

In April 2003 in Honduras 69 people were killed when clashes broke out between regular prisoners and gang members at the overcrowded El Porvenir prison near the Caribbean port of La Ceiba. It was first thought that the deaths were caused by prisoners fighting each other but an inquiry held into the deaths came up with another explanation. The inquiry found that in fact the police called to deal with the disturbance had caused many of the deaths by opening fire without warning and shooting prisoners. Ana Machado, whose son was killed, said, 'Some prisoners were still alive after the shooting and the police executed them. Others were able to save themselves by pretending to be dead.'[25]

In May another serious incident occurred in Honduras when 103 prisoners died in a fire in a prison in the northern city of San Pedro Sula. The fire broke out in a cellblock built for 50 but holding 186 prisoners. Apparently many of the prisoners could have been saved but the guards refused to open the cells in time. 'We screamed at them to let us out,' one prisoner said. 'They wanted to leave us to die,' survivors told the Honduran newspaper *La Prensa*. 'We heard them say "Let's leave these pieces of garbage to die."' The victims, many of them members of the Mara Salvatrucha street gang, either suffocated or were burned alive.[26]

The situation in the prisons in Central America and the Caribbean has been worsened by a new factor, the more determined US policy of repatriation of gang members and other convicted people to their countries of origin after they have served a sentence in a US prison. These repatriations occur with seemingly no thought as to how the poor recipient countries are going to cope with the extra demands on their social services and creaking criminal justice systems.[27]

Honduras is a poor country with an annual *per capita* income of US$947. It could be argued that it cannot afford to follow the finer points of justice and keep its prisons safe. The United States is the richest country in the world. Yet in the prisons of the United States gross abuses are also to be found. In early March 2004 an inquiry was launched into an incident in a prison in California to determine whether the guards there were guilty of criminal negligence. Ronald Herrera was a prisoner who because of his conviction for rape was held away from other prisoners in a segregation unit in Corcoran prison. He had hepatitis and kidney disease, so needed to be connected regularly to a dialysis machine. He was also seeing a psychiatrist for mental illness. One night prison officers who were at the time watching an important sports event on the television (the Super Bowl) heard howls coming from his cell. When they looked they saw that his cell window was covered with a curtain of toilet paper soaked in blood but they took no action. 'Just keep an eye on him,' the guard in charge said.

In the morning a new set of prison guards came on duty and one of them saw what looked like '"raspberry Kool-Aid" streaming out from the cell. Inside, he found Herrera slumped over on the floor, lifeless. Much of the blood had drained from his body, corrections officials said. Blood filled the toilet bowl and washed over the concrete floor of the 8-by-10-foot cell.'

Corcoran Prison has had its share of such problems. Just a week before Ronald Herrera died, three prisoners in the Security Housing Unit, where prisoners are kept in the highest security conditions, joined in a suicide pact to protest against the brutality of the guards. One of the prisoners succeeded in hanging himself. The local lawyers' group that works on behalf of the prisoners was sceptical about the outcome of the inquiry into Ronald Herrera's death. They noted that the elected district attorney who was investigating the case had received financial support from the prison guards' trade union in his election campaign.[28]

Even in the Maldives, with its image as a peaceful location for luxury holidays, violence can break out. In 2003 four prisoners died in the prison in the capital, Male, when security forces used firearms to quell an outbreak of violence.[29] Following the deaths there was an inquiry and some of those involved in putting down the disturbance were detained. The President promised that they would be prosecuted.[30]

Prisons are places where ill-treatment is common and injustices are perpetrated by officials on those held in them. But not all violence inside the walls of the prison is carried out by the prison authorities. Although the prison authorities have an obligation to protect those whom the state decides to lock up, prisons can be very unsafe places where weaker prisoners live in fear of violence from others. In England in March 2000 a prisoner aged nineteen called Zahid Mubarek was sharing a cell with another prisoner known to have racist views. During the night before he was due to be released Zahid was beaten to death by his cellmate. The attack was so brutal that the injuries made him almost unrecognizable to his family. The cellmate was subsequently convicted of murder. Zahid's family felt that their son should not have met his death in such a way while in the care of a state institution and wanted a public inquiry into how such a thing could happen. The government tried to prevent a public inquiry taking place but in 2003 the House of Lords (the highest court in England) ruled that a public inquiry should be held. It opened in September 2004.[31]

In many prison systems, rape of prisoners by other prisoners is common. In the United States an organization called Stop Prisoner Rape has been campaigning for years against this abuse. The founder of Stop Prisoner Rape was an American, Steve Donaldson, who was himself gang-raped when he was arrested and held in 1973 in a jail in Washington DC for protesting against the US bombings in Cambodia. In 2003, 30 years later, President Bush signed into law the Prison Rape Elimination Act. The law calls for the gathering of national statistics on rape in US prisons, the development of guidelines for states on how to deal with prisoner rape, the establishment of a review panel to hold annual hearings and the provision of grants to states to combat the problem.[32] Steve Donaldson died in 1996. He had been infected with HIV as a result of having been raped in prison.[33]

Corruption Thrives in Prisons

The prison guards in Quito joined the prisoners' protest by striking about their grievances. This is not surprising. Prison staff are often poorly paid, untrained and regarded with little respect. They are then an easy prey to the corruption with which many prisons are riddled. Prison staff come to work every day in a setting where corruption is taken for granted. Prisoners will be asked to pay for everything to which they should be entitled – food, a decent place in a cell, a visit from the family, a telephone call – as well as for a number of things they are not entitled to, such as drugs, mobile telephones, a place in the prison hospital when they are not sick, a trip home at night with a chance to sneak back in the morning, and a positive parole decision.

Thabani Jali is a South African judge. He was appointed by the South African government in 2001 to chair a commission to investigate corruption in the South African Correctional Service. The Jali Commission came up with some findings that showed the extent to which corruption had penetrated every corner of the South African prisons. Prisoners were leaving the premises illegally. 'One inmate enjoyed endless conjugal visits to his spouse, another stayed at various city hotels while still a prisoner.' Officers used their positions to get jobs in the department for their relatives. Prison officers were involved in drug trafficking with and for prisoners. Prison officers were taking money from prisoners in return for reductions in sentence time served, conversion of a prison sentence into a non-custodial sentence, or in return for privileges. Officers were also taking money from prisoners or their families in return for a guarantee of the prisoner's safety. Irregularities in the provision of goods and services were also found. At Grootvlei prison the commissioners found a particularly alarming situation. In addition to drug trafficking by staff and sale of prison food and other goods belonging to the state, the Commission found that young prisoners were sold to older prisoners for sexual purposes and staff were themselves sexually abusing juvenile prisoners.[34]

In the national Bilibid prison in Muntinlupa in the Philippines the Director tried to stop corruption by warning the prisoners and their families to stop giving money to prison guards. The families were unhappy with the crackdown and the Director reported that a contract had been taken out on his life as the result of his decisions.[35]

In 2002 an edition of the magazine *Judicial Gazette* caused a stir in the Dominican Republic when it published a price list of the going rate to be paid to the prison for all aspects of prison life: food, air conditioning, a room, cigars, whisky, drugs, protection, guns, authorization to see the doctor and a certificate of good conduct to get conditional release.[36]

Corruption in prisons is not confined to the poor countries of the world where prison staff are struggling to earn enough money to feed themselves and their families. Two prison officers working in the Federal Bureau of Prisons in the United States were charged with accepting bribes to smuggle cryogenic sperm kits into the minimum-security federal prison at Allenwood so that prisoners could impregnate their wives and girlfriends.[37]

The corruption that came to light in Denmark in January 2004 was somewhat unusual. In Denmark people who have been sentenced to prison may wait some time before they have to present themselves at the prison to serve their sentence. It was reported that some convicted people paid other people to do their sentence for them. The impersonators were paid up to US$180 a day to do the prison sentence.[38]

So prisons can be lawless and corrupt. What is the prison experience like for those who are sent to prison? How is it to live in prison from day to day?

Living in Prison

'I've been in prisons all around Brazil,' said James Cavallero, founder of the Brazilian human rights group Global Justice. 'They're dark, dreary, wet, and damp. Some of them feel like medieval dungeons. And it's remarkable – there's the same stench in all of them. Rotting food, urine, excrement, prisoners' sweat. That prison smell is uniform – it's teeming humanity.'[39]

Those who have never been in prison may find it difficult to imagine what it is like. At its best it can be compared with living for weeks, months, or years in a room as big as the average Western bathroom, containing a bed, chair, table, cupboard and lavatory, with a door that is locked for at least eight hours a day.

At its worst it can be rather like the experience that drove Valery Kalashnikov to claim to the European Court of Human Rights that he was being subjected to inhuman and degrading treatment because of the way he was treated in a detention centre in Magadan in the far north-east of Russia. His claim was accepted. The Court said that the conditions in which he was held for four years and ten months contravened Article 3 of the European Convention on Human Rights. Article 3 prohibits inhuman or degrading treatment. The Court judged Valery Kalashnikov's treatment to be against Article 3 because he was held in a cell where each prisoner had between 0.9 and 1.9 square metres of space. The acute over-crowding meant that the prisoners had to take it in turns to sleep. The light was on in the cell all the time and there was constant noise from the large number of prisoners. These conditions led to sleep deprivation. The ventilation was inadequate and the prisoners were allowed to smoke in the cell. The cell was infested with pests. The cell and the toilet area were dirty. There was no privacy and Mr Kalashnikov got skin diseases and fungal infections. At times he was held in the same cell as people suffering from syphilis and tuberculosis.[40]

Living in prison is rarely agreeable anywhere. Nor is it easy to predict where a prison experience would be worst. In the rich countries of Western Europe one might expect a reasonable level of humane treatment. Yet a report produced for the Justice Ministry of Portugal showed that Portuguese prisons are overcrowded, in poor condition and among the worst in the European Union.[41] In 2001 Greece was found to be in violation of Article 3 of the European Convention on Human Rights outlawing inhuman and degrading treatment because a prisoner called Peers was held in a shared cell with no ventilation and no window. Also he had to use the toilet in the presence of his cell-mate.[42]

Living in prison means being separated from friends, family and loved ones, and locked up with a group of often hostile strangers. Visits from the outside world are therefore very important to prisoners and all prison systems have some arrangements for visits. It is striking, though, how dramatic the variations are between these arrangements. In an average prison in a Latin American country, for instance, prisoners will have private visits from their partners and families, probably twice a week. The prisoners' scanty portion of their cells or dormitory will be divided by hanging sheets and cloths into little enclosed cubicles for these encounters to take place.

In the countries of the former Soviet Union the tradition is to have long visits, maybe four times a year. The family may come and stay in the prison in a small apartment for up to 72 hours and live as a family. It is very different for the prisoners from Wisconsin placed in prisons in Tennessee under a contract between the Wisconsin Corrections Department and the private prison company Corrections Corporation of America. There the requirement was that the prisoners' right to private visits should be met by contact via a videophone.[43]

In England a typical family visit to a prison might happen for one hour twice a month. The prisoner and the family would meet in a room with tables and chairs screwed to the floor. They would be watched from a control room on closed circuit television. The cameras of the system are so powerful they can read the writing on a packet of potato chips. The visitors and the prisoners sit on different-coloured chairs and the prisoners wear a sort of tabard, a waistcoat-type garment. Sniffer dogs check all the visitors for drugs. Anyone who might have been contaminated by any contact with someone using drugs in the past 24 hours will be sniffed out and sent away or told they must have their visit behind glass to prevent contact with the prisoner they are visiting.

Life Sentences

Living in prison for some means life in prison. Life sentences are imposed by many countries on those convicted of the most serious crimes. Normally this does not mean that they stay in prison for the whole of their natural life. It means that they are held until the requirements of punishment are satisfied and then the authorities assess how dangerous they are. If they are no longer felt to be dangerous they are released, often under the supervision of a social worker or other official.

In the last few years, as part of the increasing harshness of the system in many countries, there is more interest in the idea of a life sentence meaning that the prisoner stays in prison until he or she dies. In the United States now there are 127,000 life sentence prisoners. A quarter of those can expect to stay in prison for the rest of their lives. In six states – Illinois, Iowa, Louisiana, Maine, Pennsylvania and South Dakota – all those sentenced to life must serve without any hope of parole.[44] There is a prison in Louisiana called Angola. There 88 per cent of the prisoners will stay till they die. In some prisons in the United States volunteers are going into the prisons to set up hospices so that dying prisoners have somewhere less barren in which to die than a prison cell.[45]

What Happens to Dangerous Prisoners?

Life sentence prisoners are often assumed by prison administrators to come into the category of 'dangerous'. 'Dangerousness' is a controversial concept in the prison world. Some prisoners are indeed dangerous and might harm others or try to escape and cause mayhem in the world outside if they were to succeed. Others are driven to become dangerous by the brutality and cruelty of their prison experiences. Some can be dangerous in one prison environment but settle down and do no harm to anyone in another. Some are described by prison administrations as dangerous just because of what they have done. Life in prison for prisoners described as dangerous can reach an extreme of harshness. Vyacheslav, once a prosecutor in the Smolensk region of Russia, spends his days in Petak prison in Russia. Vyacheslav stabbed two women to death and stole some money. He was about to face the firing squad when Russia suddenly imposed a moratorium on the death penalty. So instead he lives in what is officially called prison number OE-256/5. The prison has been specially adapted to hold the country's most dangerous prisoners. According to a British journalist, Julius Strauss, who got permission to visit,

> Petak is as bad as it gets … the regime is so unbending and inhuman that it eventually crushes even the toughest inmates.… Petak is surrounded by water. Security is so tight that no one has escaped in living memory. The prisoners live in a state of relentless and unending despair.

The prisoners in Petak will each serve a minimum of 25 years, though they do not expect to survive that long. Half of them have TB. They live in small cells holding two people for twenty-two and a half hours a day. They spend their one and a half hour's exercise time in a small outside cage. For the first ten years of the sentence two visits a year, of two hours each, from families are allowed. Twice a year they may receive a parcel. According to Julius Strauss,

> Misbehaving prisoners are sent to punishment cells to be locked in a small, dark room with only a metal bucket and a fold-down bed for 15 days. No books are allowed. In the daytime the bed is stowed and they must stand, or sit on a tiny wooden perch a few inches wide.[46]

The Netherlands has been heavily criticized by the European Committee for the Prevention of Torture for the way it treats those prisoners who have been judged likely to escape or who must not be allowed to escape under any circumstances. These prisoners are kept in special high-security units called EBIs (Extra Beveiligde Inrichting). They can be held in these units for a period of six months, which can be extended; although after six months the prisoner can appeal against being put there and being kept there. It is a strict regime. Prisoners are allowed two ten-minute phone calls a week. Visitors to the prisoners in the EBI are subjected to a strip-search before they visit and all their conversations with the prisoners are recorded. Prisoners are normally separated from their visitors by a transparent partition but they are allowed one visit a month from their families without a partition, although physical contact is restricted to shaking hands on arrival and departure.[47]

The European Committee visited the EBI at Vught in 1996 and said that the prisoners there 'were subject to a very impoverished regime [which] was having harmful psychological consequences for those subjected to it' and noted that the regime 'could be considered to amount to inhuman treatment. To subject prisoners classified as dangerous to such a regime could well render them more dangerous still.'[48] In 2002 the European Court of Human Rights found that the treatment to which a prisoner, Van der Ven, had been subject in Vught amounted to inhuman and degrading treatment and therefore constituted a violation of Article 3 of the European Convention on Human Rights.[49] The following year the court found the same in relation to a prisoner named Lorsé.[50] The main reason for the court's finding in both cases was the routine strip-searching and particularly anal inspections carried out weekly, even on prisoners who have not left their cell since the last strip-search.

About 20,000 prisoners in the United States are kept in conditions very like those deemed 'inhuman and degrading' by the European Court. These prisoners – defined as dangerous, disruptive, violent, incorrigible, or gang members – are usually kept in prisons called supermax prisons or in units called Special Housing Units. Since the normal maximum security prisons are very secure the supermaxes have to go a lot further. Most information on life in such prisons comes from lawsuits against them. But, unusually, a professor of anthropology from Washington State was allowed in to do research in the most secure part of a supermax prison, the control units.

> Prisoners in control units ... spend 23 hours a day or more in 8-by-10 foot cells with one frosted window in the shape of a slit. They must withstand constant day-and-night clamour, raving neighbours, ghastly food, racial and other taunts, including encouragement to commit suicide, and predatory aggression.[51]

The conditions are so extreme that many prisoners lose their reason and begin to 'smear feces on cell walls, or on themselves'. 'Others take to storing their own body wastes and blood, and fashioning them into projectiles that they throw through the meals slots at guards'. The researcher discovered that prisoners found these actions 'a particularly satisfying form of resistance': perhaps, she suggested, because the guards are put in fear by the possibility of being infected with AIDS, hepatitis or other infectious diseases.

The United States has a much higher percentage of its prisoners kept in such high-security conditions than other countries.

Where Did the Idea of Prison Come from?

Prison has not always been the normal punishment for crime. Until the eighteenth century punishment was seen in a very different way. The historian Richard Evans describes a punishment scene in Berlin in 1800.

> The woman was tied down and quickly strangled, and her limbs and neck were broken by a series of blows with the heavy cartwheel wielded by the executioner. In accordance with standard practice her body was then untied and fastened to the wheel, which was placed horizontally on a long upright pole fixed into the ground next to the scaffold.... The head was cut off and stuck on top of the pole.[52]

Public acceptance of such punishments weakened as the century went on and the idea of using prisons as the main punishment for crime rather than hanging, drawing, quartering, breaking on the wheel, flogging and branding gained ground. Imprisonment meant that instead of punishing through the body, transgressors would be punished through the mind.

Thus emerged the idea of locking convicted people up in small spaces called cells in buildings with high walls, and leaving them in solitude to reflect and repent of their crimes. This tradition has clear links to Christian ideas of sin, punishment and repentance. The cells are an extension of the cells of the monasteries or convents where monks and nuns lived. This concept of the prison took over in North America and Europe during the first half of the nineteenth century and was spread round the world by the colonial powers. Thus it is possible to see in the centre of, say, Dhaka in Bangladesh or Kingston in Jamaica a British-style prison built to the same design as a prison in London or Glasgow. Such prisons were at one time used in the service of the colonial government to keep order and deal with anti-colonial movements. After independence they passed to the new governments who used them as part of the justice system they had inherited from the colonial power.

In other parts of the world, history has bequeathed a different model. In Russia prisoners were first of all banished, most of them making a journey of many thousands of kilometres. They walked for weeks or months to the distant east, where they lived in camps and worked, first for the Tsar's government and then for the Soviet Union. There was no interest in giving the prisoner a chance to think and repent. Banishment and work were the twin pillars of the system.

In China and Japan these two traditions seem to be fused. Prisoners are expected to reform and realize the error of their ways during the time they are in prison. But they must also work. In both China and Japan prisoners work for the benefit of the state, and campaigners have questioned whether the goods produced by prisoners and sold on world markets should be banned because they have been produced by captive labour.[53]

The People in Prison – Who Are They?

The type of prison may differ, depending on the country and the tradition. It may be a place holding 5,000 prisoners or one holding fewer than a hundred. It may have high forbidding walls, watch-towers and barking guard dogs. Or it may look like a hostel or residential college campus. But in many ways all prisons are the same. In particular, the people will be the same.

People in prison are not a cross-section of society as a whole. A breakdown of the population in prison in any country would not show a proportion of the professional and managerial classes, a good number of the wealthy and an equal representation of men and women, all ethnic groups, the old and the young. Most prisoners are men, young and poor. Common sense suggests that is what one would expect. Crime is mainly a man's business, a young man's business, and it is primarily from amongst the poor that those criminals most often imprisoned are recruited. In the next chapter we shall look in more detail at how acts are defined as crimes and how perpetrators of some acts are pursued by the system and end up in prison. Here we are concerned with getting a picture of the people in prison, and their main characteristics.

All over the world, prisoners come from the most disadvantaged parts of society. They are overwhelmingly poor and uneducated. They have been unemployed, suffer poor health and are often familiar with institutional life, having spent much of their childhood in children's homes, orphanages or reformatories. The prison population in England and Wales, for example, is very heavily weighted towards the most deprived and needy groups in society. According to a government report published in 2002, the people who are sent to prison are dramatically disadvantaged. They are a subset even of a disadvantaged population on every indicator. Those in prison are thirteen times more likely than the general population to have been taken into the care of the authorities as children. They are ten times more likely to have absented themselves from school and they are at least 40 times more likely to have three or more mental disorders.[54] A breakdown of the Netherlands prison population showed that about 70 per cent of prisoners were unemployed. Six out of ten had some mental disturbance and one in ten was so ill that he or she should have been in a psychiatric hospital. Half had problems with illegal drug use. A study of Swedish prisoners showed a quarter were homeless, half were unemployed and half were involved with illegal drugs.[55]

Prisons around the world are full of young men from one part of society, the poorest part. It is particularly startling to discover that in many countries prisons are also disproportionately full of men from minority groups. If the people discriminated against in a particular society are the indigenous people, then those people will be over-represented in the prison population. In New Zealand, for instance, 45.7 per cent of the prison population are Maori[56] but Maori make up only 14 per cent of the population. In Canada, in the Federal Prison System, aboriginal women make up 29 per cent of the prison population. They constitute but 3 per cent of the female population in Canada.[57]

If the people who face discrimination are distinguished by their racial group, then people of that racial group will be entering the prisons in much greater numbers. In the United States, for instance, there were more black men than white men imprisoned in 2004, although only 12 per cent of the US male population is black. Of all prisoners, 910,200 were black and 775,100 were white. Hispanics accounted for 395,400. In mid-2004 more than one in ten (12.6 per cent) of all the black men in the US aged between 25 and 29 were in prison. The comparable figure for white men was 1.7 per cent. The disproportions are similar for women in prison. Black women were nearly 4.5 times more likely to be in prison than white women.[58]

In some states the figures are even more dramatic. In the District of Columbia, for instance, the proportion of African-Americans in prison per 100,000 is 1,504 compared to 52 per 100,000 of the white population, 30 times as many. When African-Americans go

Table 1.3

**Countries with the highest proportion of women prisoners
(percentage within the prison population)**

Maldive Islands	26.6
Thailand	18.4
Kuwait	14.9
Bolivia	12.1
Qatar	11.8
Singapore	11.0
Ecuador	8.8
Netherlands	8.8
Malaysia	8.4
United States of America	8.4

Countries with the lowest proportion of women prisoners

Liechtenstein	0
Tanzania	0.9
St Kitts and Nevis	0.9
Burkina Faso	1.0
Malawi	1.2
Gambia	1.2
Seychelles	1.3
Zambia	1.5
Jordan	1.6
Sudan	1.7

Source: These statistics were taken from *World Prison Brief Online*, 28 June 2005. Statistics are not necessarily from the same year but represent the most recent figures available. Percentages have been rounded.

for a job, most employers assume they are ex-prisoners unless they have a certificate proving they do not have a criminal conviction.[59]

In Western Europe prison populations are swelled by large numbers of foreigners, people seeking asylum or immigrants from poorer parts of the world. In Austria, Estonia, Italy, Malta and the Netherlands, a third of all the prisoners are foreigners. More than four out of ten prisoners in Belgium are foreigners.[60] There were so many Romanians in Austrian prisons that in January 2004 Austria reached agreement with the government of Romania to build and run a prison in Romania to house Romanians held in Austrian prisons who were either convicted or had admitted a crime.[61]

Women in Prison – Few and Far Between

Most prisoners everywhere are men. Women in prison represent on average but one in twenty of all prisoners. However, the average conceals wide differences. Some countries rarely imprison women, while in others the proportion of women prisoners is growing rapidly. In the United States, for instance, the number of men in prison has increased by 3.3 per cent a year on average since 1995. The number of women has increased by an average of 5 per cent a year.[62] In England and Wales, between 1992 and 2002 the men's prison population increased by half whilst the population of women in prison increased by 173 per cent.[63]

The women in prison are especially disadvantaged and find being in prison particularly painful. In February 2004 publicity was given to a report from the Human Rights Commission of Canada that criticized the treatment of women prisoners in Canada. Citing statistics, the Commission says the 'reasons women offend, their life experiences and their needs are unique'.[64] Eighty per cent of women in prison in Canada report prior abuse. They have high rates of mental and physical disability, experience significant poverty and have higher unemployment rates than their male counterparts, the report says.[65]

We know many things about the women in prison in England and Wales: 37 per cent had previously attempted suicide; around 40 per cent could have been diagnosed as harmful or dependent users of drugs; as many as half had been victims of domestic violence; and up to a third had been victims of sexual abuse.[66] So they have not been well cared for or protected before they become prisoners. The prison system of England and Wales has been scarred in the past few years by a substantial increase in the number of women prisoners committing suicide, 61 in the past decade. One such case was eighteen-year-old Sarah Campbell, who died in 2003 from an overdose of tablets on the first day of her sentence. The inquest jury found that the prison failed on six counts to care properly for Sarah.[67] After her death her mother, Pauline Campbell, became a one-woman protest movement against the self-inflicted deaths of women in prison. She demonstrated outside any prison where there had been such a death and tried to stop the prison transports bringing in new prisoners. She has been arrested several times.[68]

Women's prisons are sometimes portrayed as gentler than men's, with women having more space and better conditions, sleeping in clean dormitories with embroidered bed covers. Indeed, women's prisons are often less crowded and less brutal. But women prisoners are not necessarily protected from the brutality that can be the rule in some male prisons. In Austria in March 2003 a violent incident took place in a women's prison. Seventy police, mostly men and armed with guns, batons and shields, carried out a training exercise in the prison. They made the women stand facing the wall while their cells were ransacked. Then they marched the women to the prison chapel where they forced them to strip naked and submit to a body search. One prisoner said: 'I was forced to take all my clothes off and then bend over next to a fellow prisoner while the officers examined me intimately to see if I had hidden drugs on me. As far as I know there was no reason for them to even suspect this.'[69]

Prisons can be dangerous places for women. Although all the international rules about running prisons make it clear that women should be guarded by women and protected from sexual abuse, many are assaulted and abused. In June 2004 a woman from Dallas, Texas, who had been serving four years for a drug offence in a prison camp run by the US Federal Bureau of Prisons, was awarded $4 million in damages because she had been raped by a prison officer, Michael Miller. According to reports, the 47-year-old woman was assaulted after she went for a urine test. She told the court that, as he was raping her, Michael Miller told her, 'Do you think you're the first? This happens all the time.' Other employees at the prison camp told the court that Ms X had been a model prisoner and had never flirted with the officers. The woman explained her reasons for taking the case. 'It's never been about the money,' she said. 'It's always about justice. I want things to change at the prisons. I want security cameras at officers' stations and intercom systems in cells and on the compounds, so inmates can make emergency calls and things like that won't happen anymore.' The officer continued to work as a guard after she reported him but he was transferred to a men's prison. He is under criminal investigation.[70]

Sexual abuse is also widespread in many other countries. The US State Department reported that in Pakistan in 2003 many children in prison were born to female inmates who were sexually abused by prison guards.[71]

Sexual humiliation can also be part of serving a prison sentence, with frequent internal body searches and little privacy when bathing or showering. In Kenya it is reported that sanitary napkins were not provided and the women had only one set of clothes, so that when they were washing their clothes they were left naked.[72]

In many ways women suffer more from being imprisoned than men do. Prison systems are designed for dealing with men. Men are the majority everywhere. Policies, rules and regulations are formulated with men in mind. Since the number of women is much smaller, in some countries there is one women's prison and all the women prisoners from the whole country are held there, even though it may be many hours' or days' journey from their home districts where their families live. An alternative model is to establish small women's units or wings attached to a number of larger male prisons but separated from them. Under this system the women, both staff and prisoners, are usually the poor relations, with least access to facilities.

Although most of the women in prison present no danger and do not need to be kept in conditions of high security, often the same security regimes apply to women as to men. Women's prisons are an afterthought and some makeshift building is found with little space for exercise, or other activities. The education and training programmes emphasize the requirements of men prisoners and women prisoners are usually offered little more than a tailoring workshop, for example, producing uniforms for the prison system, or cleaning work. A group of women prisoners serving life sentences told the Canadian Human Rights Commission: '[W]e are starved for vocational training … [and] told that the best they can do is give you a mop, broom and a spatula.'[73] In the San Miguel Penal Centre in El Salvador 72 women, convicted of all offences from the most minor to murder, live together in one long room with one toilet. They sleep in bunks one above the other and are locked into the room between six at night and six in the morning.[74]

Separation from children is a source of constant pain to many imprisoned mothers. If they can keep their children with them, they worry about bringing them up in such an environment. The *Pak Tribune* reported in 2004 that in Pakistan

> health facilities are almost non-existent in women's prisons. Almost all rape victims who become pregnant end up delivering while still jailed for a crime not committed. They have no access to pre-natal care, are under-nourished and over-worked in jail and ultimately end up delivering in the unhygienic prison health care facility under pathetically sub-optimal conditions. Obviously this results in a dis-proportionately high number of infant and maternal deaths in a country which already has a dismal infant and maternal mortality rate.[75]

Should Children Be in Prison?

It is not just the children of women prisoners who find themselves in prison. Many countries use prisons to lock up troubled children even though they pay lip service to the United Nations Convention on the Rights of the Child, which says very clearly that children should be imprisoned as a last resort and for as short a time as possible. All over the world children are being locked up in prison-like facilities – sometimes called re-education centres, training centres or reformatories, but prisons in all but name. The United Nations Children's Fund (UNICEF) estimates that at any one time over one million children are deprived of their liberty in some institution.[76] Most of these children will be poor, from the street or from a background of abuse and misery.

In Asunción in Paraguay there was an infamous children's prison called Panchito López juvenile detention centre. It burnt down in July 2001. At the time of the fire it was holding 240 young people, though it was built to hold 80. Nine out of ten of the children had not been convicted but were awaiting trial. They started the fire to draw attention to the conditions there. A journalist who had visited reported that each child got as much personal space 'as that covered by a newspaper'. In some of the cells they had to sleep three to a bed and temperatures could stay at around 40°C for weeks on end.[77]

The treatment of children and young people in the Youth Training Center in Nevada in the United States was so bad that the Justice Department in Washington DC had to intervene. The Justice Department found that the young people were punched in the chest, kicked in the legs and pushed against lockers and walls. They were thrown to the floor, slapped in the face, had their heads smashed into doors, and were pulled to the floor from their beds. When they wrote letters to alert people outside to what was going on, the letters were censored. They were put into isolation without any safeguards against misuse. Psychotropic drugs were overused. When they were being transported outside the facility they were handcuffed to each other. The Justice Department and the State of Nevada entered into an agreement in 2002 to reform the practices at the Center.[78]

A stay in a children's prison or reformatory is a very good predictor of what will happen to the child in later life. Many of the inhabitants of adult prisons spent some of their childhood in these establishments and learnt that their place in the world order was to be a criminal and an outcast of no further interest to respectable society.

Prisons Are Bad for Health

If prisons can be unjust and dangerous, they can also be very unhealthy. In September 2004 two prisoners in Quezon City jail in the Philippines died of tuberculosis. Another 26 were also ill with the disease. An official said, 'Once inside the jail, it is only a matter of time before a patient's condition – specially those with TB – deteriorates.' Overcrowding and poor conditions are blamed for the deaths. Local councillors called the conditions at the jail 'subhuman' and said that prisoners 'often' died there. It is not surprising that the conditions are bad. The Quezon City jail was built to hold 400 people. At the time of the deaths it was holding 3,000.[79]

Quezon City is not the only place where a prison sentence becomes a death sentence. In many countries of the world rates of infection from TB, HIV–AIDS and hepatitis B and C are much higher in prisons than in the community outside. TB can be 100 times more common in prison than outside and HIV infection can be 75 times more likely in prison than in outside society.[80] Such deaths can happen in rich countries, too. A report on the treatment of HIV-positive prisoners at the Limestone Correctional Facility in Alabama in the US found that the deaths of almost all the 44 such prisoners who had died since 1999 could have been prevented. The doctor who studied the deaths said that a number of prisoners were allowed 'to drown in their own respiratory secretions and suffocate' whilst others died of 'AIDS-related malnourishment'.[81]

Many of the people who go to prison are those who cannot afford the medicines they need, who come from housing conditions that breed tuberculosis, and who may have worked in the sex industry and contracted HIV infection. The living conditions in most prisons of the world produce ill-health even in those who come to prison in reasonable shape. The buildings are overcrowded. The threat of violence hangs over everything. Light and fresh air can be minimal. Poor food and infection-spreading activities such as tattooing and unprotected sex are common.

Many prison systems have great difficulty dealing with the infrastructure problems, such as inadequate sewerage, that arise from many human beings confined in a small space with overused sanitary facilities. Some systems lack a regular water supply.

Health care in many prisons is minimal. Doctors cannot be found who want to work in the prisons. Medicines are not provided and, if they are, they are often sold rather than supplied to meet need. Prison hospitals are often cells just slightly less crowded than normal cells.

Because certain drugs are illegal many of those who use them end up in prison. Treatment is not available and the drug use continues. Needles are scarce in prison and drug users are desperate. When injecting they share needles and their infections spread. In February 2004 the United Nations Development Programme reported that in Kyrgyzstan drug users who share needles account for 80 per cent of the country's HIV cases. More than half of the 364 HIV cases reported in Kyrgyzstan in 2003 could be traced to just one prison in the Osh district. To combat this problem, the country has introduced a needle-exchange programme, aimed particularly at the prisons.[82] In most countries of the world, though, needle exchanges are not allowed in prisons.[83]

Mental illness and prisons are intertwined in several ways. Many of those locked up in prison are suffering from a range of mental conditions. They should be in hospital rather than prison. Living in prison can have a bad effect on mental health and lead to depression and suicide attempts. In 2004 the Correctional Association of New York published a study of how mentally ill prisoners were treated in the prisons of New York State. The report painted a grim picture.

On nearly every site visit we encountered individuals in states of extreme desperation: men weeping in their cells, men who had smeared feces on their bodies or lit their cells on fire, prisoners who cut their own flesh, inmates who rambled incoherently and paced about their cells like caged animals....[84]

Working in Prisons – What Sort of Job Is It?

In January 2005 a gruesome discovery was made in a vehicle parked just one kilometre from a Mexican maximum security prison, the Matamoros Penitentiary. Inside the vehicle were the bodies of six prison guards. They had been shot dead. Some of them had been blindfolded before they were murdered.[85]

The most famous prison in Brazil was probably Carandiru in São Paulo. In October 1992 the quelling of a disturbance at Carandiru cost the lives of 111 prisoners. Carandiru prison was demolished in 2002 in a symbolic move to show that the prison system in São Paulo was set for change. Dr Drauzio Varella worked in the prison for 13 years as a volunteer doctor and wrote a book about his experiences.[86] He describes the life of the prison guards. They are paid very little. Those that 'respect honesty' have to do a second job as a security guard at night. Their working hours are long. Those on the night shift leave at seven in the morning and go straight to their other job. Those on the day shift just get a nap at work and see their beds at the weekend. In order to cope, many drink heavily. 'Alcoholism and obesity are very common.... It is not easy to be with them.'[87]

Working in prisons is rarely a well-paid, prestigious job. Prison guards are sometimes conscripts working in prison during their compulsory military service period. Others are aspirants to join the police who did not have enough qualifications. Few have proper training for the job and many feel it is the sort of work to keep quiet about, nothing to be proud of. A woman prison guard from a prison in Rajasthan said to researchers from the Indian Penal Reform and

Justice Association, 'When I meet people outside they look at me and say … what kind of place have you chosen to work in – it only houses the lowest of low!'[88]

When prison staff hear about prisoners' rights and perhaps have to go on a training course about them, they tend to wonder when some attention will be paid to *their* lack of rights. The researchers from the Indian Penal Reform and Justice Association noted that 'The staff always complain that nobody asks about them.… They feel more organizations ask about prisoners than them.'[89]

Life after Prison – How Easy Is It?

So what happens to people when they leave prison? Do they leave with their problems solved and their minds made up not to return to a life of crime? In fact, leaving prison is not easy. A woman who had been released from a prison in Australia said after five months outside, 'I often feel I've got "ex-prisoner" stamped on my forehead.'[90]

Those who had homes and work before they went to prison often lose them. Those who had families may become estranged. Prison seems to leave a mark on them. Leaving prison is not easy anywhere. It is certainly not easy in Russia, where poverty has become widespread. It was not easy for 38-year-old Oleg Tikin. As an ex-prisoner he could not obtain the all-important documents every Russian needs to get legal housing and work. So he

> roams a grim post-Soviet twilight world, living in train stations or apartment building lobbies, dodging frequent police round-ups. 'I can't get a *propiska*,' he says, referring to a police stamp in his internal passport granting permission to live in Moscow. 'This means no job, which means no home, which means the cops can arrest you any time.'[91]

In the United States being an ex-prisoner is a particularly difficult status. It is estimated that 630,000 people leave US prisons every year. Wherever they return to, they face barriers to taking up their lives again. A criminal record prevents them from taking up many jobs. In 14 states almost all criminal convictions are listed on the Internet for anyone to see. Some states ban people with certain convictions from public housing. Driving licences can be suspended or revoked in 27 states for some drug offences.[92]

Many states – Florida is one of them – have laws that prevent people convicted of felonies (more serious crimes) from voting, sometimes for a few years and sometimes for life. Currently this affects about five million people – but its effects spread more widely. Many people are not sure if they have lost the right to vote or not, so they stay away from the polls.[93] And the people these laws affect are disproportionately African-Americans, who represent 12 per cent of the US population and 40 per cent of those who have lost the right to vote. According to Brent Staples, writing in the *New York Times*, 'Republican operatives have deliberatly used scare tactics with this group of voters – most of them Democrats – in the hope of keeping them home on Election Day.'[94]

What Is American 'Exceptionalism'?

In this respect the penal policy of the United States is exceptional, as it is in many other ways. A new phrase has been coined by commentators, 'American exceptionalism'.[95] It is used to describe a range of policies of the United States. In the crime field it means that developments in crime policy in the United States are quite outside the framework adopted by other countries. These developments have moved in a direction so extreme that the United States is seen as an aberration, not sharing a common tradition with other Western countries.

One person who has suffered from this new approach is Brian Smith. He was in Los Cerritos shopping mall in Los Angeles when he was caught on a security camera standing near two women who were stealing some sheets. He did not know the women and he did not steal anything himself. The women were sentenced to two years in prison for stealing the sheets. Brian Smith was convicted of assisting them and, since he had been convicted before (of purse snatching in 1983 and burglary in 1988), he was sentenced under the law called 'three strikes and you're out' which entails a minimum of 25 years and a maximum of life imprisonment.

By September 2003 California was holding over 7,000 people under this rule. They included Richard Morgan, who was sentenced to 25 years for shoplifting a baseball glove; Herman Clifford Smith, 25 years for trying to cash a forged cheque for $193; Gilbert Musgrave, 25 years for possession of a stolen video recorder; George Anderson, 25 years for filing a false driving licence application; Johnny Quirino, 25 years for stealing razor blades, and Eric Simmons, 25 years for possessing three stolen ceiling fans. Under the three strikes law, 25 years means 25 years. Prisoners have no chance of parole.[96]

We saw, above, that in earlier centuries criminals were hung, drawn and quartered; huge crowds gathered and rushed to dip a cloth in the blood of the executed person as a talisman.[97] America's attitude to punishment can sometimes have an echo of these earlier times. This is the only framework in which we can understand a discussion that took place in 2004 in the Senate of the State of Utah about how prisoners condemned to death should be executed. What was the right method to use? The purpose of the bill was to ban execution by firing squad in favour of lethal injections. A Democratic senator called Ron Allen, speaking in favour of the bill, said that allowing murderers to choose firing squads meant they could 'go out in a blaze of glory'. Perversely this made heroes of criminals and caused victims' families more pain, he said. He was opposed by a Republican senator called Dave Thomas, who said media circuses are 'exactly what we want' in executions. 'We don't want these sentences to be carried out in the dead of night so no one knows,' he said, adding that lethal injection was painless and 'the easy way out'.[98]

Even severe mental illness is no bar to execution. In 2004 the Governor of Texas, Rick Perry, refused an appeal against a death sentence in the case of Kelsey Patterson. Kelsey Patterson was a paranoid schizophrenic. He had shot and killed two people in 1992. After the shooting he took off all his clothes except his socks and stood in the street shouting until the police came and arrested him. At his trial he assured the court that devices had been implanted in him that made him act against his will. He had previously spent time in mental institutions. Most unusually, the Texas Board of Pardons and Parole had recommended to the Governor that the death sentence should not be carried out. But the Governor denied the request 'in the interests of justice and public safety'.[99]

May Williams (not her real name) is a white 24-year-old with brown hair and brown eyes. She weights 160 pounds. On 12 November 2004 she began two years' probation supervision for possession of cocaine. She has (January 2005) stopped reporting to her probation officer and is now classed as an 'absconder/fugitive'. Publicity is something that those who are convicted in the US have to accept. All the information about May Williams including her real name (which is not being used here) is on the Internet. Unlike the practice in other countries, prison and probation departments in the US put details of their convicted offenders and prisoners on the Internet. Anyone from anywhere may visit the website of, say, the Florida Department of Corrections and choose any crime category, for example, drug crime. The database then provides information on everyone, in prison or on probation, most of them with photographs, names and alias, fingerprint class, current prison history, prison number, date of birth, release date, prison where currently held or probation office in charge of the supervision, and crimes for which convicted.

The United States is exceptional in many other ways, too. Until 2005, people who committed their crimes when under the age of eighteen were liable to the death penalty. In that year the Supreme Court ruled against the execution of those who committed their crimes when juveniles. The US is probably the only country in the world to sentence those who committed their crime when under the age of eighteen to life imprisonment with no prospect of release. The State of Michigan has 146 people serving life without parole for crimes they committed between the ages of fourteen and sixteen.[100]

The United States has gone much further than any other democratic country in accepting the view that punishment should be as it was in the eighteenth century, an expression of total state power and a dramatic public event that serves to illustrate a victory in the contest between good and evil.

How Much Imprisonment?

This approach in the US is seen not just in its extreme punishments but in the amount of punishment it imposes on its citizens. In July 2004 another milestone was passed. Imprisonment rates are usually measured per 100,000 of the general population. The world average is about 143 per 100,000. The West European average is 108 per 100,000. The new figure for the United States for the end of 2004 was 724 per 100,000.

What can we make of these figures and the huge differences between countries? The US keeps six times as many of its people in prison as does the country on its borders, Canada. The United States has 4.6 per cent of the world's population and 23.1 per cent of the world's prisoners. Canada has 0.51 per cent of the world's population and 0.4 per cent of the world's prisoners.

The differences across the world are very great. The differences within regions are also remarkable. Spain, for instance, is one of the highest European imprisoners at 139 for every 100,000 people in Spain. Yet in France, a similar country in terms of size and socio-economic level, there are 91 per 100,000. In Africa, similarly, Botswana has a rate of 339 while Lesotho, close by, has a rate of 143. The explanation for these differences is that different countries

Table 1.4

World's 10 highest imprisoners (prison population rates per 100,000 of the national population)

United States of America	724★
Russian Federation	550
Belarus	532
Turkmenistan	489
Cuba	487
Suriname	437
Belize	420
Ukraine	416
St Kitts and Nevis	415
Maldive Islands	414

World's 10 lowest imprisoners

Burkina Faso	23
Nepal	29
India	29
Nigeria	31
Gambia	32
Mali	34
Sudan	36
Republic of Guinea	37
Indonesia	38
Monaco	39

Middling imprisoners – a selection

Latvia	339
Chile	241
Libya	207
Uzbekistan	184
New Zealand	168
UK: England and Wales	143
Australia	117
Canada	116
Turkey	95
Finland	71

Source: These statistics were taken from *World Prison Brief Online*, 28 June 2005. Statistics are not necessarily from the same year but represent the most recent figures available. Percentages have been rounded.

★ Latest figure (end 2004).

make different choices about how to spend their money and place a different value on punishment.

If Imprisonment Is an Unjust System, Does It Matter?

Many readers who have got this far may be beginning to react. Questions may be coming to mind. We are talking here about prisoners. These are people who have committed crimes. It is all very well to be so concerned about prisoners, but what about their victims? They may well sympathize with some Irish hospital patients. In Ireland in March 2004 a fracas broke out in a hospital accident and emergency department after members of the public waiting for their treatment discovered that, whilst they were waiting, a prisoner had been seen and treated immediately. A group of patients shouted abuse at the prisoner as, handcuffed to an officer, he went to the head of the queue. 'One witness said a group of patients began shouting abuse at the prisoner, calling him a "scumbag", before staff were forced to step in and break up the group.' The doctor at the hospital defended the system, saying that 'Prisoners are entitled to their human dignity as well. It is not appropriate for them to be paraded in handcuffs in a public place. They are already serving time for their crimes.' The real problem, apparently, was shortage of staff and beds at the accident and emergency unit rather than a decision to give priority to prisoners.[101]

Such a response is understandable. Prisoners are not popular and do not get much public sympathy anywhere. Certainly many of those in prison have committed crimes. When someone is convicted of a crime there has to be a response. Otherwise the rule of law is weakened. Prison is a reasonable punishment to show society's disapproval of law breaking.

So why should we care if prisons are lawless and violent and the number of prisoners keeps rising? We should care for a number of reasons. To tease out these reasons it is necessary to look a little more deeply at the process, to consider how people get to prison. It is worth asking why prisons seem to hold mainly the poor and the marginalized. Are the poor more criminal, or just more likely to be punished? Is prison a benign social institution making a real contribution to keeping people safe? Or does it usually create injustice, brutalize and embitter those held, and thus make crime worse? These are the questions addressed in the next chapter.

Notes

1 From <http://barbados.allinfoabout.com/glendairyonfire.html>, originally in *The Nation*.
2 'Fifteen Hostages Freed in Ecuador', BBC News, 18 February 2004.
3 'Jail Hostage Crisis Grips Ecuador', BBC News, 7 April 2004.
4 'Fifteen Hostages Freed in Ecuador'.
5 'Jail Hostage Crisis Grips Ecuador'.
6 'Ecuador Jail Hostage Crisis Over', BBC News, 15 April 2004.
7 'Ecuador Jail Protests Turn Bloody', BBC News, 24 June 2005.
8 Judge Sachs in the case of *August and another v Electoral Commission and others* 1999 4 BCLR 363 (CC) at pp. 372–3.
9 The Honourable Louise Arbour, *Commission of Inquiry into Certain Events at the Prison for Women in Kingston*, Public Works and Government Services Canada, Ottawa, 1996, p. 179.
10 US State Department, *Country Reports on Human Rights Practices – 2003, Angola*, Washington DC: 2004.
11 'Dhaka Central Jail Crammed Full of Prisoners', *Star City*, 5 April 2004.
12 US Department of Justice, *Prisoners in 2004*, Washington DC: Bureau of Justice Statistics, 2005.
13 Council of Europe, *Report to the Portuguese Government on the Visit to Portugal Carried Out by the European Committee for the Prevention of Torture and Inhuman or Degrading Treatment or Punishment from 19 to 30 April 1999*, Strasbourg, July 2001.
14 Fiona Macaulay, 'Political and Institutional Challenges of Reforming the Brazilian Prison System', Working Paper Series, University of Oxford Centre for Brazilian Studies, 2002, p. 4.
15 Andrew Coyle, 'Prison Reform and the Management of TB in Eastern Europe and Central Asia', in Vivien Stern (ed.), *Sentenced to Die: the Problem of TB in Prisons in Eastern Europe and Central Asia*, London: International Centre for Prison Studies, 1999, p. 55.

16 Quoted in Moscow Centre for Prison Reform, *In Search of a Solution: Crime, Criminal Policy and Prison Facilities in the Former Soviet Union*, Moscow: Human Rights Publishers, 1996.

17 Michael Marks and Philip McLaughlin, 'Investigative Report into the Deaths of Seven Vermont Inmates and Related Issues', Vermont: Agency of Human Services, 13 March 2004.

18 Her Majesty's Prison Service, *Local Prisons – the Way Forward*, conference report, London, September 2002.

19 See *Robert Napier v the Scottish Ministers*, Court of Session, Edinburgh, P739/01.

20 Council of Europe, *Report to the Hungarian Government on the Visit to Hungary Carried Out by the European Committee for the Prevention of Torture and Inhuman or Degrading Treatment or Punishment (CPT) from 5 to 16 December 1999*, Strasbourg, March 2001.

21 See *Annual Reports of Her Majesty's Prison Service 1994–2004*, Home Office, London.

22 *Hansard*, House of Commons, Written Answers 4 July 2002, Col. 530W.

23 Becky Branford, 'Brazil's "Medieval" Prisons', BBC News, 2 June 2004.

24 'Two Dead, Five Injured in Prison Uprising in Northeastern Brazil', Associated Press, 26 June 2005.

25 'Police Blamed for Jail Riot Deaths', BBC News, 12 May 2003.

26 'Guards Accused over Honduras Fire', BBC News, 18 May 2004.

27 See Anna Cearley, 'Deportees Are Linked to Mexico Crime Rate, Tijuana Police Blame US Felons for Robberies, Kidnappings and Killings', *San Diego Union Tribune*, 12 September 2004; and Council On Hemispheric Affairs, 'Honduras' Response to Violence Made It Worse', press release, 10 September 2004.

28 Mark Arax, 'California Prisoner's Gruesome Death Probed – Investigators Want to Know if Guards, Who Were Watching the Super Bowl, Were Negligent', *Los Angeles Times*, 9 February 2004.

29 'Fourth Maldives Prisoner Dies', BBC News, 29 September 2003.

30 Frances Harrison, 'Maldives Inmates "Held Unfairly"', BBC News, 30 January 2004.

31 Extensive information on this case can be found on the inquiry website, <www.zahidmubarekinquiry.org.uk>.

32 Stop Prisoner Rape, 'Prison Rape Elimination Act Becomes Federal Law', press release, 4 September 2003.

33 Stop Prisoner Rape, 'Stephen Donaldson, 49, Led Reform Movement Against Jailhouse Rape', press release, 19 July 1996.

34 *The Jali Commission of Inquiry: Report to Be Presented to the Parliamentary*

Portfolio Committee on Tuesday 20 August 2002, Pretoria, South Africa.

35 *Philippine Daily Inquirer*, 8 August 2003.

36 'El Negocio Penitenciario', *Gaceta Judical*, 125 (25 January–8 February 2002), pp. 10–12.

37 ABP News, 10 October 2000.

38 Julian Isherwood, 'Rich Danish Criminals Pay Stand-ins to Serve Sentences', *Daily Telegraph*, 30 January 2004.

39 Becky Branford, 'Brazil's "Medieval" Prisons'.

40 *Kalashnikov v Russia*, ECHR, Application no. 47095/99, 15 July 2002.

41 Alison Roberts, 'Portuguese Prisons "Worst in EU"', BBC News, 17 February 2004.

42 *Peers v Greece*, ECHR, Application no. 28524/95, 19 April 2001.

43 *Contract with CCA, Wisconsin Legislative Fiscal Bureau Report*, Wisconsin: Department of Corrections, January 2001.

44 Marc Mauer, Ryan S. King and Malcolm C. Young, *The Meaning of 'Life': Long Prison Sentences in Context*, Washington DC: The Sentencing Project, May 2004.

45 See the website of the National Prison Hospice Association based in Boulder, Colorado, <www.npha.org >.

46 Julius Strauss, 'Waiting for Death in Russia's Alcatraz', *Daily Telegraph*, 10 August 2004.

47 *Lorsé and others v the Netherlands*, ECHR, Application no. 52750/99, 4 February 2003.

48 Council of Europe, *Report to the Netherlands Government on the Visit to the Netherlands Carried Out by the European Committee for the Prevention of Torture and Inhuman or Degrading Treatment or Punishment (CPT) from 17 to 27 November 1997*, Strasbourg, September 1998.

49 *Van der Ven v the Netherlands*, ECHR, Application no. 50901/99, 4 February 2003.

50 *Lorsé and others v the Netherlands*.

51 Peter Monaghan, 'Madness in Maximum Security', *Chronicle of Higher Education*, Vol. 50, Issue 41, 18 June 2004, p. A14.

52 Richard J. Evans, *Rituals of Retribution: Capital Punishment in Germany, 1600-1987*, Harmondsworth: Penguin, 1997, p. 194.

53 See Vivien Stern, *A Sin against the Future: Imprisonment in the World*, Harmondsworth: Penguin, 1998, Chapter Five.

54 Office of the Deputy Prime Minister, *Reducing Re-offending by Ex-prisoners, Report by the Social Exclusion Unit*, London 2002.

55 International Centre for Prison Studies, 'Analysis of International Policy and Practice on Reducing Reoffending by Ex-Prisoners', report for the Social Exclusion Unit, London, 2001 (unpublished).

56 Department of Corrections, *Census of Prison Inmates and Home*

Detainees 2003, New Zealand, 2004.

57 Canadian Human Rights Commission, *Protecting Their Rights: a Systemic Review of Human Rights in Correctional Services for Federally Sentenced Women,* Ottawa, 2003, para. 1.2.

58 US Department of Justice, *Prison and Jail Inmates at Midyear 2004*, Washington DC: Bureau of Justice Statistics, 2005.

59 See Marc Mauer, 'Thinking about Prison and Its Impact in the Twenty-First Century', *Ohio State Journal of Criminal Law* (2005), pp. 607–18.

60 Marcelo F. Aebi, *Space I (Council Of Europe Annual Penal Statistics),* Strasbourg: Council Of Europe Survey 2002, 23 June 2003.

61 Public Services International Research Unit (PSIRU), *Prison Privatisation Report International, No. 60, January/February 2004,* London: University of Greenwich.

62 *Prison and Jail Inmates at Midyear 2004.*

63 Fawcett Society's Commission on Women and the Criminal Justice System, *Women and the Criminal Justice System*, London, 2004, p. 5.

64 Canadian Human Rights Commission, *Backgrounder 2,* recommendations of the special report *Protecting Their Rights: a Systemic Review of Human Rights in Correctional Services for Federally Sentenced Women,* Ottawa, 2003.

65 Canadian Human Rights Commission, *Protecting Their Rights: a Systemic Review,* paras 1.1–1.7.

66 Prison Reform Trust, '"Buying Time": Crisis Management of Women's Prisons', press release, 11 March 2004.

67 Helen Carter, 'Inquest Blames Jail for Overdose Death', *Guardian*, 25 January 2005.

68 'Prison Deaths Protester Arrested', BBC News, 19 June 2004.

69 Michael Leidig, 'Austrian Minister in Jail Search Gaffe', *Daily Telegraph*, 18 March 2004.

70 Toni Heinzl, 'Rape Victim Wins Suit Against Prison Guard', *Fort Worth Star-Telegram*, 4 June 2003.

71 US State Department, *Country Reports on Human Rights Practices – 2003, Pakistan,* Washington DC, 2004.

72 US State Department, *Country Reports on Human Rights Practices – 2002, Kenya,* Washington DC, 2003.

73 Canadian Human Rights Commission, *Protecting Their Rights: a Systemic Review,* para. 6.1.5.

74 'Deacon Serving in El Salvador Finds Hope behind Bars', *The Record*, Episcopal Diocese of Michigan, November 2004 .

75 Shazia Rafiq, 'Justice and Equality for Women', *Pak Tribune*, 12 April 2004.

76   United Nations Children's Fund, *Justice for Children: Detention as a Last Resort – Innovative Initiatives in the East Asia and Pacific Region*, Bangkok: UNICEF, 2004, p. 4.

77   *The Wire* (Amnesty International magazine), 31, 6 (September 2001).

78   *Criminal Justice Newsletter*, Washington DC: Pace Publications, 1 April 2004.

79   Tina Santos, '26 QC Jail Inmates Found Afflicted with Tuberculosis', *Philippine Daily Inquirer*, 9 October 2004.

80   Vivien Stern, 'Problems in Prisons Worldwide, with a Particular Focus on Russia', *Annals of the New York Academy of Sciences*, New York, 2001.

81   *Corrections Journal*, Pacecom Incorporated, 24 May 2004.

82   Canadian HIV–AIDS Legal Network, *Prison Needle Exchange: Lessons from a Comprehensive Review of International Evidence and Experience*, Toronto, 2004, pp. 41–2.

83   This point is discussed further in Chapter 5.

84   Correctional Association of New York, *Mental Health in the House of Corrections: a Study of Mental Health Care in New York State Prisons*, June 2004, p. 54.

85   'Mexican Prison Guards Shot Dead', BBC News, 21 January 2005.

86   Drauzio Varella, *Estação Carandiru*, São Paulo: Companhia das Lettras, 1999.

87   Quoted in People's Palace Productions, *Staging Human Rights 1: Interim Report*, Queen Mary, University of London, May 2002 p. iii.

88   Rani D. Shankardass and Saraswati Haider, *Barred from Life, Scarred for Life, Experience and Voices of Women in the Criminal Justice System*, Gurgaon, India: Penal Reform and Justice Association (PRAJA), 2004, p. 105.

89   *Ibid.*, p. 145.

90   Dot Goulding, *Severed Connections: an Exploration of the Impact of Imprisonment on Women's Familial and Social Connectedness*, Perth: Murdoch University, 2004, p. 23.

91   Fred Weir, 'Putin Faces Many Challenges in Bid to Drastically Cut Russia's Poverty', *Canadian Press*, 28 March 2004.

92   Legal Action Center, *After Prison: Roadblocks to Reentry, a Report on State Legal Barriers Facing People with Criminal Records*, New York, 2004.

93   Christopher Uggen and Jeff Manza, 'Democratic Contraction? Political Consequences of Felon Disenfranchisement in the United States', in *American Sociological Review*, 6, 6 (December 2002).

94   Brent Staples, 'How Denying the Vote to Ex-Offenders Undermines Democracy', *New York Times*, 17 September 2004.

95 See Michael Tonry, *Thinking about Crime: Sense and Sensibility in American Penal Culture*, Oxford: Oxford University Press, 2004.

96 Dan Glaister, 'Buried Alive under California's Law of "Three Strikes and You're Out"', *Guardian*, 8 March 2004.

97 See Richard J. Evans, *Rituals of Retribution: Capital Punishment in Germany, 1600–1987*, Harmondsworth: Penguin, 1997.

98 'US State Moves to End Firing Squad Executions', <www.ananova.net>, 20 February 2004.

99 *Criminal Justice Newsletter*, Washington, DC: Pace Publications, 1 June 2004, pp. 5–6.

100 Marc Mauer, Ryan S. King and Malcolm C. Young, *The Meaning of 'Life'*, p. 19.

101 Siobhan Maguire and Dearbhail McDonald, 'Anger over Prisoners Jumping A & E Queues', *Times*, 21 March 2004.

2

Crime and Its Definition: How Just Is Criminal Justice?

Since crime does not exist as a stable entity, the crime concept is well suited to all sorts of control purposes. It is like a sponge. The term can absorb a lot of acts – and people – when external circumstances make that useful. But it can also be brought to reduce its content, whenever suitable for those with a hand on the sponge. This understanding opens up for new questions. It opens up for a discussion of when enough is enough. It paves the way for a discussion of what is a suitable amount of crime.

Nils Christie, 2004[1]

Do Prisons Make Society Safer?

In the first chapter we had a look at the prison, an institution that is used by every country of the world, an institution that continues to be taken for granted and rarely questioned in spite of the problems it presents. Many countries are building more prisons and filling them up until they become as overcrowded as the old prisons were before. The process continues even though the problems, violence and injustices created by imprisonment are well known and well publicized.

Prisons stand at the end of the process of dealing with crime. Prison will be there to deal with those who are, it is decided, a threat to others, so that the threat can be removed. Prison exists to hold those people whose actions stop others living free from crime and free from fear. All may not be well within the high walls of the prison, but for those outside, the high walls, the watchtowers and maybe also the stories of dreadful happenings within are symbols of the power of the state to punish. They are a reassurance to the public that they will be protected from people who prey on them and threaten public peace.

But prisons might not have lasted so long if they were only symbolic. There is also something very practical about them as a solution to the problem of crime. The argument is very obvious. There has been much debate about the catchphrase 'prison works'. Politicians use it to defend their penal policies. Critics question it and summon arguments. It defines the debate. In one sense, of course, prison does work. A prison is a prison. People who would do harm to others are locked away so that they cannot carry on doing that harm. Whether prisons are unjust and violent inside, whether they make the people who go to them better or worse, need not concern the law-abiding citizen. One thing is sure. Prisons protect society by holding people who would otherwise be outside, stealing, robbing, terrorizing, smuggling, causing damage and spreading fear.

So prisons – with their grey walls, watchtowers, razor wire and brooding blocks with small barred windows – symbolize the maintenance of law. They keep locked away people who would do harm to others. More than that, they also prevent crime in another way, so the theory goes. Prison is such a grim place and loss of freedom is a very harsh punishment. People do not want to lose their freedom and the thought of being sent to prison stops the potential law-breaker committing a crime that would otherwise have been committed. The existence of the prison punishment *deters* people from committing crime.

It is also argued by some that prisons can be good places, serving a useful purpose. They can be places of reform where criminals go in as bad people and come out a little better. Being sent to prison will teach them a lesson so they will give up crime. Or possibly being sent to prison will give them a chance they never had before to learn a trade, give up taking illegal drugs or get educated, and then they will give up crime.

These are the basic arguments. They are powerful arguments that can be heard in the speeches of many a politician or commentator. They can be read in the newspapers of the world every day. They will be quoted by people interviewed by television journalists. They will say, 'I am happy for more prisons to be built whatever it costs so that more criminals can be locked up and then we shall be safer.' When people are convicted and not sent to prison, perhaps given an order to do community work instead, there can be an outcry.

If we want to make the case for a different crime policy, a policy that mends people rather than damages them, and strengthens communities rather than fracturing them, we need to show these arguments are wrong. That requires some analysis. What is the connection between crime and punishments, between levels of crime and harshness of punishment? What actually causes crime and what is likely to reduce it? How much protection comes from prisons and other punishments? Maybe crimes are reduced if a country has harsh punishments, maybe not. Perhaps the countries which lock up a lot of their people in prison are the safest countries. Perhaps, on the other hand, they are the more dangerous ones.

To answer these questions we must go back to the beginning of the crime story. If prisons are at the end of the line, the crime that is committed and leads to a conviction and penalty is at the beginning. So in this chapter we will look at some questions about crime and consider what we know. We will try to pin down how we can know how much crime there is and who suffers from it. What impact does crime have on different groups of people? Who are the main victims? It is also worth considering what causes crime rates to change. Perhaps they rise when times are hard, because people need to steal to eat. Perhaps on the other hand they rise when times are good, because there are more goods to steal. In some countries alcohol plays a large part. When there is more money for alcohol there may be more alcohol-induced violence. It is often asserted that crime is caused by poverty. Others would say that crime rates rise when a shared poverty is replaced by competition and inequality.

When we come to think about crime itself, then there are matters of definition to be considered. Who defines an action as a crime? How is crime measured? How easy is it to compare crime rates between different countries?

Measuring Crime – Is It Easy?

Trying to measure crime is not easy. Definitions of crime vary and some actions are crimes in one country and not another. But there is considerable agreement across many different societies about the core criminal acts. As was said earlier, sexual assault, robbery and theft are all described as crimes in the criminal laws and penal codes of the world. Murder and all forms of personal violence are deemed to be crimes, though in many societies violence against women is taken less seriously than other forms of violence, and committing violence against children is often permitted by the criminal code as a parental right. In England much controversy arose about a new law governing whether parents could hit their children. One side argued that parents should not be allowed to hit their children. The opponents maintained that parents had a right to punish their children by hitting them within reason. After much discussion in Parliament a compromise law was passed. Parents could hit their children, but they would be breaking the law if they hit them so hard that it left a red mark.[2]

However, it is worth stepping back a bit and looking at how an act moves from possibly coming under the definition of a crime into becoming an actual crime. Many acts take place every minute of every day that could be described as crimes. People hit each other. People threaten violence to others. Men lean out of their car windows in stressful driving situations and threaten to kill other drivers. Property is taken unlawfully. Workers defraud their bosses. Citizens defraud the government. Taxpayers cheat the tax department. Sexual activity takes place involving those below the legal age for such activity.

Many human interactions can be defined as criminal acts if someone wants to do so. A mother loses her temper and beats her child. At some point the beating crosses a line and could be defined as child abuse. Two young men who are good friends have too much to drink. One insults the other and it ends in a fight. One of them gets a bruised and bloody face. He has been a victim of assault. However, his friend who caused the bruises will argue that he was acting in self-defence because he was being threatened with a bottle. Children coming home from school see a group of children from another school. For years these two schools have been hostile to each other. They get into a fight. Some of them get bruises. Then they go home arguing about who won and vowing to seek revenge the following day. Is this to be defined as schoolchildren fighting as schoolchildren have always done? Or is it involvement in group violence, or conspiracy to wound, which is in some jurisdictions a serious crime? An old lady has dementia. Her dementia makes her violent. She attacks her elderly husband with a kitchen knife and he is cut quite seriously. Is this act going to be defined as a crime and is the old lady going to be arrested by the police and taken before a judge? A dishevelled person with low-level mental disturbance walks up the street shouting incomprehensible but hostile words at passers-by. Does he need compassion, help and the offer of a place where he can get a hot meal and a bath? Or should he be arrested, charged with being a public nuisance and locked up?

All day, every day, such actions take place. All of them could be classified somewhere as a crime. But few are. Most are resolved through discussion, family intervention, various forms of social interaction or mediation. None of the parties involved decides that what has happened must be classified as a crime and therefore goes to the police and starts the process that can lead to arrest, charge, trial, conviction and punishment. Either these acts are ignored and seen as just part of life, or another solution is found.

The Creation of Crimes

What leads a range of bad, anti-social or problematic acts to be defined as criminal acts, to be dealt with by criminal proceedings? It depends. One way of turning problematic acts into crimes is for societies that used to regulate themselves to become more modern. Being more modern means having a police force. An old man in an Indian village told Mark Tully, the BBC journalist:

> [T]he worst thing that has happened is that the police started coming into the village. In the old days the police never came – we used to sort out our quarrels ourselves or with the *panchayat* (village council). But nowadays people keep running to the court or the police station. They waste a lot of money and achieve nothing.[3]

In societies that are becoming industrialized, people no longer know and trust each other. In consequence, many acts that were regulated by community life have to be regulated another way. When community regulation is replaced by more modern structures the system is formalized and crime is used more often to define and shape the response to unwanted acts. When developed societies change in other ways the same process takes place. Unwanted acts that were seen as social problems or health problems are defined instead as offences against social conformity and turned into crimes.

Mrs Patricia Amos lives in England. She is a mother with three daughters. She has had problems in her life. She had one kidney removed and became addicted to painkillers. She then started taking heroin, but after a while she tried to change her life by undertaking treatment. The treatment was successful and the drug problem was over. But her situation got worse when her family life fell apart. Because of her problems, so she told an interviewer, she had not taken her responsibilities seriously enough. She had let her own mother be the mother of her daughters. Then one day the daughters came home from school to find their grandmother lying on the floor. She died 24 hours later.[4] After that one of the daughters, Jackie, became very unhappy and would not go to school. In 2001 not sending your children to school in England became a crime that carried the punishment of prison. Mrs Amos was sent to prison because the court listened to her story and decided that she had not tried hard enough to get her daughter Jackie to go to school.

Between 1997 and 2003 in England and Wales more than 660 new crimes were created.[5] In the United States also new crimes are created frequently. In fact various right-wing groups are arguing that society is becoming 'over-criminalized'. A conservative think tank, the Cato Institute, has published a book called *Go Directly to Jail: the Criminalization of Almost Everything*. Examples quoted are that of a 12-year-old girl taken off in handcuffs for eating French fries in a metro station[6] and a law making it a crime to wear low-slung trousers.[7] The book concludes that, 'it is now frighteningly easy for American citizens to be hauled off to jail for actions that no reasonable person would regard as crimes'.

Who Can Be a Criminal?

So acts that previously were not crimes, such as not sending your children to school or downloading certain images from the Internet, can become crimes. There is another way that more acts can become defined as crimes. Acts can become crimes depending on the person who commits them. The same act committed by a child of six and an adult of 26 will be seen differently. Whether the act of a child who does something wrong, for example hitting another child or stealing from a shop, becomes a criminal act depends

Table 2.1

**Minimum age at which children are subject to penal law in
selected countries with 10 million or more children under
18 years old**[8]

Bangladesh	7
India	7
Nigeria	7
Pakistan	7
South Africa	7
Thailand	7
United States	7★
Indonesia	8
Iran	9★★
Philippines	9
UK (England)	10
Ukraine	10
Russian Federation	14
Vietnam	14
Egypt	15

★Age determined by state, minimum age is 7 in most states under common law.

★★Age 9 for girls, 15 for boys.

Sources: Children's Rights Centre Country Reports (1992–6); Council of Europe, *Juvenile Justice and Juvenile Delinquency in Central and Eastern Europe,* 1995; United Nations, *Implementation of UN Mandates on Juvenile Justice in the Economic and Social Commission for Asia and the Pacific (ESCAP)*, 1994; Geert Cappelaere, Children's Rights Centre, University of Ghent, Belgium.

entirely on where the child lives. The age at which an act committed by a child can be described as a crime depends on the 'age of criminal responsibility' in the law of each country.

Different approaches to crimes committed by children were graphically illustrated in the early 1990s by two events that took place, one in England and one in Norway. In England two small boys were accused of beating to death a two-year-old boy. They were aged 10 at the time. The whole process by which they were dealt with resembled very much what would have happened to an adult. They were charged. They were held in custody before their trial. Their trial was not in a juvenile court but in an adult court and in public. They were given a little platform to stand on so that the people in the court could see them. After the trial they were sentenced to a minimum of ten years in custody. More than 300,000 people signed petitions saying the time served should be longer. The time was subsequently increased to 15 years by an elected politician, the Home Secretary. The European Court of Human Rights criticized both the trial procedure, which it rejected as unfair, and the sentencing procedure, which allowed a politician not a judge to make the decision about length of time to be served.[9] Eventually, after long legal proceedings, the boys were released in 2001, having served eight years, and a judge made an order preventing the media publishing any information about their whereabouts.

In Trondheim in Norway at about the same time a similar tragedy happened. In 1994 a five-year-old girl called Silje was beaten and left to freeze to death in the snow. Two six-year-old boys confessed to beating her and leaving her in the snow. After a week the two boys were back at the kindergarten. Counsellors were brought in to work with all involved. The police, the girl's mother and people in the area agreed that punishment was not appropriate. Silje's mother said, 'I feel sympathy for them. They need compassion.' She believed it was easier for her to deal with the death of her child if she felt kindness rather than vengeance. The emphasis of the response was to prevent the two boys growing up to become dangerous. And the way to achieve that was to keep them integrated in the normal environment.[10]

As Nils Christie says, 'Crime is one, but only one, among the numerous ways of classifying deplorable acts.'[11] In some places whether or not an act is a crime depends on whether the act is committed by a man or a woman. In Nepal until 2002 it was a crime for women to have abortions. The woman who had the abortion committed the crime and the punishment ranged from three years to life imprisonment. Twelve women who were serving prison sentences when the law was repealed were released in 2004 after pressure from women's rights groups.[12] In 2002 there were many protests about the sentence imposed on Amina Lawal Kurami, a woman in her thirties from northern Nigeria, who was given the death penalty for committing adultery. An Islamic court sentenced her to be stoned to death. However, her former lover faced no punishment. Fortunately the protests were successful. She was acquitted on 25 September 2003.[13]

Acts can become crimes or not depending on the mental state of the person committing the acts. Mental illness in many countries is regarded as reducing the person's responsibility for a criminal act. The consequences are then to be sent to a place of treatment, a hospital, rather than a place of punishment, a prison. As we saw in the case of Kelsey Patterson (Chapter 1), in the US mentally ill people who kill someone can be convicted of murder and be sent to prison. In Arkansas they can be executed. A man called Charles Singleton, a diagnosed schizophrenic, 44 years old, was given a death sentence two decades ago for murdering a grocery store assistant called Mary Lou York. Since he was mentally ill he stayed on death row and his condition worsened. Then the authorities in Arkansas had an idea. He was forcibly given powerful drugs to alleviate the symptoms. His lawyer appealed against the forcible medication. On 10 February 2003 the Third Circuit Court of Appeals held that the State of Arkansas could continue to medicate Mr Singleton – knowing that the idea was that he might become sane enough to be executed. In January 2004 he was given a lethal injection in the state's death chamber.[14]

If Charles Singleton had killed a person in the Netherlands he would most likely not have been convicted of a crime at all. Because of his illness he would have been locked up in a secure clinic and looked after by medical professionals.

So we can see that talking about crime and crime rates is a bit more complex than measuring the number of certain acts committed for which someone is convicted in a court. The process of turning an unwanted bad act into a crime punishable by the criminal law depends on how a society is organized, its values and culture, the importance of law as opposed to traditional structures, and the amount of money available for a criminal justice system. Urbanization can mean that acts that people do not like and cause harm may be described as crimes and dealt with through the machinery of the criminal law, rather than being dealt with by the community in another way. More crimes can be created. More people can be brought within the area of the criminal law, so that what they do can be classified as a crime rather than as a symptom of illness or, in the case of a child, the failure of the family or society to bring the child up properly. The amount of crime in a society is the result of individual actions but also of policy choices made by the government.

Measuring Crime Levels Is Difficult

Measuring crime, therefore, is not just a question of counting the number of murders, rapes, robberies, thefts and other illicit acts coming to the knowledge of the police in a particular place. It also has to take into account the social context and the political view taken of crime and criminals. Even when these are taken into account, and even in countries where crimes are clearly defined in the laws and there are highly developed statistical offices, problems still occur in assessing the amount of crime in any country. Crime statistics are only a rough and ready guide.

Take an imaginary example. A woman comes home and finds a window in her house open and some cash missing from the place in the kitchen where she keeps a little money for emergencies. Will this event end up in the crime statistics as another housebreaking or not? That depends. The first question is, was it a break-in at all? Did she leave the window open and one of her family who knows about the emergency money and had a cash crisis climbed in and took it, intending to pay it back? If she is sure the money has really been stolen will she tell the police? That depends. If she has insurance and wants to get some money back from the insurance company then she has to tell the police. When people get their possessions insured, levels of crime reporting are much higher. Some people even increase the value of what was stolen to get more money from the insurance company. If she lives miles from the police station and a long way from a telephone she might not think it worthwhile to report it.

Her attitudes to the police are an important factor. If she is poor and sees the police as unfriendly or oppressive she will probably not report it. If the police have a reputation for sexually harassing women at the police station she will probably not report it. If she knows that her neighbour had a similar break-in, did report it, spent hours at the police station filling in forms when she should have been at work, and the police did nothing, then she will probably not report it.[15]

If we change the scenario and look at what might happen if the woman had come home and found a man hiding in the house, who had then sexually assaulted her, the question of whether the crime would be reported becomes even more complex. In some countries the shame would be too great for women even to think of reporting such an act. In other countries the way the police would respond to the woman if she went to report it might be so unsympathetic that she would feel it was not worth going through further trauma. In fact, the way the crime of sexual assault is reported is an interesting indication of the interaction between crimes committed and crimes reported. If there is a police reform the police may be told they must no longer treat women complaining of sexual assault with suspicion. They may be told that they can no longer suggest that the woman is making up her complaint or that she probably encouraged the man to make advances and changed her mind later. They may be prevented from suggesting that she is actually the one at fault because she was wearing a short skirt. The system may be changed and policewomen may be employed instead of men to deal with such complaints. There may be a special part of the police station set aside for women only, staffed by specially trained people. The result may be that women at last feel it is worth reporting sexual assaults. The number of such crimes in the official figures may rise considerably and it may seem that there is a great increase in violent crime when this is not the case.

Domestic violence is another hidden crime. A study of physically abused women showed that in Bangladesh two-thirds of the women kept the violence entirely to themselves. They did not tell anyone about it. Not one of the more than 10,000 women who were questioned reported the violence to the police. In Egypt fewer than half told no-one and not one of them told the police. In Cambodia the same survey found that only one in a hundred told the police. Even in Canada, where measures to stop violence against women are very progressive, only one in four reported the violence they had suffered to the police.[16]

So, when states start taking domestic violence against women seriously it will appear that the number of violent crimes has increased considerably. In fact women have just become more prepared to report that they have been attacked by their husband or partner because they know they will be heard. In Peru in 1993 a new law increased the protection against domestic violence and established special 'women police stations' where women could take their complaints of domestic violence. A number of cities opened such specialized police stations and other towns created specialized units in ordinary police stations. When the new law came in the number of cases that were reported increased and in 1996 it reached a new record of 6,294 cases.[17]

The official crime figures of any country are the end product of a long list of uncertainties and complexities like these. Also, the police have considerable control over what crimes are recorded as crimes and may well have an interest in less than accurate recording. If, for instance, their performance is measured by how many crimes they solve they have an interest in recording those easy to solve and not recording those where they fear they will not get a result. A Russian Vice-Minister of Justice said in 1998 that overcrowding in his pre-trial prisons was caused by pressure on the police.

> [T]heir performance is measured by the number of crimes they uncover and elucidate. In Moscow, for example, the current level of crime exposure is 92 per cent. The vast numbers of people spending time in SIZOs [pre-trial prisons] for petty crimes may be explained by the practice of investigating officers of remanding suspects in custody because they are keen to meet performance targets and raise their quota of crime clear-up rates, particularly in competition with their fellow investigative officers. On the whole, I do not place great faith in official crime detection and clear-up rates.[18]

So it is not surprising that surveys carried out in both the United States and the United Kingdom asking a large sample of people if they have been a victim of crime always show that much more crime is experienced than is actually reported to the police.

Comparing Crime Rates in Different Countries

However, measuring and comparing crime rates between countries can be done and is done. In recent years the International Crime Victim Survey has been carried out in many countries from all regions of the world. Experts see it as more reliable than comparing crime figures from different countries because it is based on interviews, either by telephone or in person, with a representative group of residents of each country who are all asked the same questions about crime and being a victim.[19] So the results do not suffer from the differences in the way police collect statistics or in the way governments decide to present them. They do of course reflect what those answering the questions have defined for themselves as a crime.

The results of the survey carried out in 1999 in 17 industrialized countries showed that the risks of having your car stolen were highest in England (2.6 per cent of victims per year) with Australia

Table 2.2

Comparative homicide rates per 100,000 of the population in selected countries, 1999–2001

Australia	1.87
Bulgaria	3.87
Canada	1.77
Denmark	1.02
England and Wales	1.59
Estonia	10.60
France	1.73
Finland	2.90
Japan	1.05
Lithuania	10.60
New Zealand	2.50
Northern Ireland	2.70
Norway	0.95
Russia	22.10
Scotland	2.20
South Africa	55.86
Turkey	2.67
USA	5.56
European Union average	1.60

Source: Gordon Barclay and Cynthia Tavares, *International Comparisons of Criminal Justice Statistics, 2001*, London: Home Office, 2003.

next.[20] Having your car broken into and some object stolen – for example a radio, a bag or the car mirror – was most common in Poland (9 per cent of victims a year).[21] Having your car damaged was most common in Scotland (12 per cent).[22] The crime that Japanese were most likely to face was having a bicycle stolen (8 per cent). Australians were most likely to have their house burgled or experience an attempted burglary (7 per cent).[23] The chances of being attacked in any way were highest in Australia, England, Canada, Sweden and Finland (over 3 per cent). In Japan assault was very rare (0.4 per cent).[24]

Table 2.3

Comparative homicide rates per 100,000 of the population for selected cities, 1999–2001

Amsterdam	3.10
Ankara	2.55
Belfast	5.60
Berlin	2.30
Copenhagen	1.81
London	2.60
Moscow	18.38
New York	8.65
Ottawa	0.94
Paris	2.00
Prague	4.33
San Francisco	8.10
Stockholm	2.84
Sydney	1.63
Tokyo	1.21
Vienna	2.80
Washington DC	42.90

Source: Gordon Barclay and Cynthia Tavares, *International Comparisons of Criminal Justice Statistics, 2001*, London: Home Office, 2003.

Looking at all the 17 countries, the most common crimes involve cars. Four in ten crimes involved stealing, damaging or stealing from cars. In Catalonia and Portugal about six out of ten crimes involved cars. In Japan four out of ten crimes involved stealing bicycles or motor-bikes.[25]

People's feelings about crime were surveyed. There was a high level of agreement. The most serious crime for the majority was having your car stolen and not getting it back. The second most serious was felt to be sexual assault.[26]

Some crimes are more likely to be recorded by the police than others. Since murder is so serious, homicide rates are usually quite reliable and are often compared to give an indication of levels of violence in different countries. All the statistics show enormous variations in murder rates. The United Nations records that in 2000 Colombia had a murder rate of just less than 70 per 100,000, while Botswana had a rate of one per 100,000.[27] Among Western countries, the United States with 5.56 homicides per 100,000 of the population has more than three times the rate of Canada with 1.77 homicides per 100,000.[28]

So what can we conclude so far? We can see that crime levels can be a creation. There is a fixed centre: violence, murder, robbery, where the statistics are probably reflective of reality. But crime figures overall will be a creation of governments. Governments can create more crimes; and can decide to ask their prosecutors to prosecute more acts as crimes rather than illnesses or social problems or nuisances. They can decide to implement a policy called zero tolerance where every little infraction of the most minor law is prosecuted. The possibilities are there for the business of dealing with crime to grow. We can also conclude from looking at the homicide rates that violent crime levels vary dramatically from less than one per 100,000 in Norway to nearly 56 in South Africa and from less than one in Ottawa, Canada, to nearly 43 in a city only 960 kilometres away, Washington DC. We shall be considering the implications of these differentials later in this chapter.

A Biased System?

We have seen that the process of defining and dealing with crime is malleable. The ideology and policies of the government can make a great difference to how much is spent on crime control, what priority crime control has in decisions on social spending and how much non-conforming behaviour will be tolerated, managed or responded to in non-criminal ways.

The next area we need to consider is how the criminal justice system operates. What is the connection between crimes and punishments? What factors come into play as the system first of all defines crime and then moves to punish it? Those who are victims of a crime may not stand an equal chance of getting redress. All those who commit crime may not get treated equally when the crime is prosecuted.

In fact, the evidence shows that the people at the lower end of society are least likely to be protected from crime, the least likely to get redress when crimes are committed against them, and the most likely to suffer from injustice within the criminal justice process. This bias against the poor is to be found to some degree in all countries of the world and has a long history. The historian Richard Evans noted that in the 1830s and 1840s in Germany, those questioning the morality of the death penalty were becoming 'increasingly disturbed by the fact that the vast majority of the offenders who went to the scaffold … were powerless and poor'.[29] A campaigning pamphlet noted: 'The death penalty … is applied almost exclusively against the proletariat.'[30] When the death penalty came to be less frequently invoked in eighteenth-century England new punishments were sought. Eventually one was found: transportation to Australia. The first shipload of convicts to set sail for Australia in 1787 also contained a high proportion of the least fortunate in society. Thomas Chaddick was driven by hunger to steal twelve cucumbers. He was transported, as was an unemployed woman, Elizabeth Powley, who stole bacon, flour, raisins and butter. An 82-year-old woman who dealt in rags and old clothes was on the ship, as was a nine-year-old chimney sweep. Nearly half of the convicts on the ship were labourers.

When it comes to defining crime and the punishments that go with the crime, different standards apply. In the UK, when the poor take more social security benefits than they are entitled to claim, they can be sent to prison. When the rich avoid tax they are likely to get a visit from a tax inspector, with a deal being struck to pay the money back in instalments. When an ordinary individual drives a car absentmindedly and someone gets killed, even when there was no harm intended, the individual will usually go to prison. If a company has dangerous machines and a worker gets killed, the company may have to close the factory and pay fines but rarely will a specific individual be found guilty and punished.

Who suffers most from crime? Who are most likely to be victims of crime? Most people would expect that those with most possessions are most likely to be attacked and robbed; that the houses of the well-off will be broken into most often. In fact, the evidence shows that crime bears most heavily on the poor, all over the world, in the North and the South. Certainly the poor have little worth stealing, but stealing from them is easier. Those who can afford it protect themselves from crime. Some people live in a house in an African city surrounded by a high wall and guarded by watchmen day and night. Others live in a Western city in a gated community where a security guard stops all those entering, checks their destination and then rings up the person they are visiting to check if a visitor is expected. Many houses in the United States have an unwelcoming little signboard on their front lawn. It warns any intruder that the householder is connected to a security company that provides 'an armed response'. Wherever they find themselves, those who can buy security are safer.

The poor are more likely to be victims of certain crimes. Figures from the United States show that households where the income is under $7,500 a year have nearly seven burglaries for every 100 households. Those with income over $75,000 have just over two burglaries per household. The poorer you are, the more you fear going out at night. Of those earning over $50,000 a year just over one in four was afraid of going out at night in their neighbourhood. Of those earning under $20,000 a year, half feared to go out.[31]

Furthermore, the effects of being a victim of crime can be more devastating. If a wealthy man has his car stolen he reports it to the police and the insurance company and is offered another car to drive in the meantime by the insurance company. When a poor woman who needs to get her produce to the nearest town to sell it has her bicycle stolen, her livelihood goes too.

At the point where a crime might lead to investigation and prosecution many forces come into play. If the woman whose bicycle has been stolen reports her loss to the police no good may come of it. She may even regret it because the bribe that is required may be greater than the cost of another bicycle. 'If a poor man is beaten by a rich man and goes to file a case against the rich man, the officer concerned does not even register the case,' said one poor man from Bangladesh.[32]

When the single mother in a public housing development in England has her few belongings taken from her home she cannot claim on the insurance because she has no insurance, either because she cannot afford it or because the area has such a bad name that her home is uninsurable. The police may be less assiduous in finding the burglar because they concentrate their protection efforts on wealthy areas where the wealthier people are more vocal in expecting good policing. The poor are more likely to get police attention not when they are victims but when they are suspects.

The Poor and Policing

In 1999 the World Bank carried out a major study of the meaning of poverty to the people that suffer it. The study was published as *Voices of the Poor*. People in 50 countries were interviewed and asked about their lives and how they saw their situation. Insecurity and crime was one of the themes. It found that the poor are less well protected by the institutions of criminal justice and by the police. It is the police who should be the first port of call for victims of crime, and they should also be front-line workers for a peaceful community. Yet the World Bank report notes how widespread is bad experience of the police. The report comments, 'In countries as different as Jamaica, Uganda, India and Moldova, police brutality is mentioned as a serious problem facing the poor.'[33]

In 2002 the United Nations Development Programme (UNDP) and the Bangladeshi government produced a report on the police force in Bangladesh. Bangladesh is regarded by Transparency International as the most corrupt country in the world and the UNDP report shows that the police there are regarded as one of the most corrupt bodies. The police are seen by the public as more interested in extortion and bribery than in crime fighting.[34] In 2004 the Governor of Morelos State in Mexico sacked all the detectives in the police force, 552 of them, because they were allegedly protecting a drugs gang. Federal police came in to take over their duties.[35]

In countries where the police are not generally corrupt, bias creeps in another way. The places where the poor live are disproportionately policed. Certain groups are profiled as likely to contain more criminals and they then attract more police attention. Racial profiling is a contentious issue, with US civil rights groups arguing that the police concentrate on certain groups, stopping them more often. A study carried out in Texas in 2002 found black motorists who were stopped were 1.6 times more likely to be searched than white motorists.[36]

How Do Poor People Fare When the Case Comes to Court?

After the police have done their work comes the court trial. There is much evidence that the poor are disproportionately punished. A number of different factors come into play that account for this. One is corruption. Instead of judging the case on the rights and wrongs, the judge makes a decision influenced by who pays the most. The judge might even dismiss the case if he or she is paid enough. *Voices of the Poor* comments that, 'In Madagascar the police and judges, who are supposed to be the guardians of justice, are seen as the most corrupt.'[37]

Voices of the Poor also tells of a man in Moldova who had been in hospital for seven months following a brutal beating in the street. 'Despite the fact that the police had helped him, he decided not to pursue the case when his attackers threatened his life. They even gave him 80 lei with the demand that he bribe the judge to dismiss the case.'[38] In the end he did what they asked. What else could he do? In Zambia in 2004 the Chief Justice suspended two magistrates. One was suspected of taking money from a suspect. Another was reported as having driven around in a car that had been held by the court as evidence in a criminal trial.[39]

Judges in many legal systems may decide whether or not an accused person is released on bail or kept in prison. In 2004 a high court judge in Bangladesh was sacked after a judicial inquiry found he had probably taken money to arrange bail.[40] Judges also have to decide whether an accused person is guilty or not. (In other systems that role belongs to the jury.) That decision can be influenced by corrupting the judge: paying money so that the decision comes out in favour of the person who paid, or in favour of the one who can pay the most.

Bribery can also be used to influence the sentence. Even when it is impossible for a corrupt judge to find someone not guilty, perhaps because there were many witnesses, there is the possibility of corruption at the sentencing stage. The judge may announce that the guilty person is to be sent to prison, but then add that the sentence will be suspended so that the convicted person will not actually go to prison. Or the judge may decide that the best punishment for the convicted person is an alternative sentence such as community work. In Kenya an investigation into judicial corruption chaired by a High Court judge was presented to the Chief Justice in October 2003. Statements had been sent to the investigation by nearly 1,000 people. It found evidence against five out of the nine Appeal Court judges, 18 out of 36 High Court judges, 82 of the 254 magistrates and 43 out of 2,910 paralegal officers. The report suggested that the judges were operating a price list, charging nearly K$200,000 for a successful outcome at the Court of Appeal, up to K$20,000 at the High Court, up to K$17,700 for a favourable verdict for a murder or armed robbery charge and up to K$6,360 to get off a manslaughter, rape or drugs charge. Presenting the report to the Chief Justice, the investigator, Mr Justice Ringera said, 'We are apprehensive that in handing over to you the report we are presenting to you a dragon. It is bound to snort, jump, kick and even attack for corruption always fights back. Your Lordship will have no option but to seize it by the horns and slay it.'[41]

In systems where bribery is not usually found the process can be biased against poor people in other ways. For example, wealthy people accused of a crime can look around for the most skilful and well-regarded lawyer, never mind the cost. They can buy the services of the lawyer, hoping that the lawyer will convince the court that they are not guilty or, if the evidence of guilt is over-whelming, will argue successfully for a lighter punishment. For people without money it is not so easy. The State of Louisiana in the USA was the subject of a damning report on how far access to justice was available to all. The report found not enough funding for defence lawyers for poor people. It found political interference with the system. The lawyers provided to poor people were badly trained and not well supervised. The report concludes, 'Without adequate defence services ensuring a fair day in court, the social fabric of our democratic way of life begins to erode.'[42]

Many poor people end up in prison because the sentence they are given is a fine and they have no money to pay. The person with means can pay. The poor cannot. The punishment is not prison. It is to pay money to the court. But the punishment for not paying the fine is prison. All they have is their freedom and that is taken instead of money. So the poor person will end up in prison when the wealthier person who committed the same offence and paid the fine will not.

Unfairness does not always come from corruption or lack of resources for poor defendants. Sometimes the judge is swayed by worthy motives but the outcome is still biased against poor people. The people in front of the judge in the courtroom may be homeless and live on the street. They may need to be seen by a doctor. At least, thinks the kindly judge, once they are in prison, then they will have a roof over their heads. They will get hot food. There will be a medical service to deal with the health problems. Surely, thinks the judge, that is the right thing to do. Lock them up and at least they will get help. Sometimes the judge genuinely wants to pass a sentence other than prison but that sentence depends on the convicted person having a permanent and stable home. The non-prison punishments can sometimes involve a form of supervision that can only take place when the person lives in a home with a telephone.

The Laws Can Be Biased, Too

In 1997 an African-American man appealed to the US Supreme Court against his ten-year prison sentence for distribution of crack cocaine. He argued that the sentence was unfair because the law itself was racially biased. He lost his appeal. Sometimes the laws have built into them a bias against certain groups of people. For many years campaigns have been carried out in the United States against the law that lays down the punishments for possessing cocaine. In the 1980s crack cocaine became a hot political issue when it became linked to violence. Its use was thought to be rife in the inner cities and very addictive. New laws were passed in 1986 and 1988 making punishments for involvement with crack cocaine much more severe than for powder cocaine, even though the physical reactions to both are very similar.

For powder cocaine the required sentence for possessing and intending to distribute it is five years' imprisonment for 500 grams or more. For crack cocaine the five-year sentences are imposed for only five grams. Also, only crack brings an automatic five-year prison term for a first offence of possession with no evidence of intent to distribute. For five grams of powder cocaine the sentence could well be probation.

The main users of crack cocaine are poor black people. Powder cocaine is used more by wealthier white people.[43] According to the Citizens' Commission on Civil Rights:

While progress has been made in recent decades to address racial disparities in employment, housing and other aspects of American life, racial inequality in the criminal justice system is growing, not receding. A primary cause and visible manifestation of that inequality is the well-known 100-to-1 ratio in federal law that dictates widely divergent sentences for crack cocaine and powder cocaine offenses. African-Americans feel the sting of this irrational policy since they are almost exclusively targeted for federal crack cocaine prosecutions.[44]

Racial disparity in sentencing in the United States, according to a recent report, is 'surreptitious'.[45] It is usually not blatant and overt, but built into the system. The report summarizes how the discrimination works. First of all, unemployed people are subject to harsher sentencing, but unemployed black and Latino young men are sentenced more harshly than unemployed young white men. Suspects who are held in detention before their trial are likely to be more severely sentenced, and black and Latino defendants are more likely to be held in detention pre-trial. Black people who are accused of harming white victims are sentenced more harshly than black people who harm other black people or white people who harm other white people. Black and Latino people charged with less serious crimes such as drug or property crimes get more severe sentences.[46]

Many studies of the operation of the death penalty in the United States show bias against African-Americans. In cases where the murder victim is white the convicted person is more likely to receive a death sentence.[47]

Amnesty International reported in 2004 that the use of the death penalty in Singapore against those found with illegal drugs disproportionately affects the 'most marginalized or vulnerable members of society. They include young people who are just entering adulthood, drug addicts, the poorly educated, the impoverished or unemployed, and migrant workers.'[48]

Even a Good Criminal Justice System is a Limited Way to Control Crime

We see, therefore, that many of the criminal justice systems of the world are themselves unjust, biased against the poor and against minorities, insensitive to women and neglectful of children. They protect the rich and ignore the needy. They are inefficient and corrupt. They are part of the crime problem rather than part of its solution. Yet it is accepted that a criminal justice system that works effectively is essential for the maintenance of the rule of law. It must ensure that people are prosecuted, and fairly and proportionately punished. It must protect society from those who would threaten it. No-one should be above the law and there should be no impunity for certain people.

A fair criminal justice system is essential and we say more about its shape and nature in Chapter 5. Even when the police are not corrupt, the courts are fair, the punishments are rehabilitative and social reintegration after prison is provided, the effects of the punishment system on crime control and crime reduction is limited. How much crime there is and how safe a society is do not depend on the criminal justice system. The huge differences we saw in murder rates (Tables 2.2. and 2.3 above) are not related to how efficient the police are, how many people go to prison and whether or not the death penalty is used. They are related to social and economic factors in each society. The criminal justice system plays a very small part.

Why is the effect of the criminal justice system so marginal? First of all, it is because punishments do not reform those who receive them. Punishments are important because they show society's disapproval of cruel and damaging acts and can protect society from dangerous people, but the punishments used in most countries most of the time do not change the recipients. According to available figures the majority of people, worldwide, who serve a prison sentence leave prison and are convicted of another crime. Within two years of being released from prison, 59 per cent of all prisoners discharged in 1999 in England and Wales were convicted of another crime. The figure for young people under the age of 21 was even higher. Nearly three out of four of these had been convicted again by the time two years was up.[49]

The Correctional Service of Canada analysed 50 studies involving 336,052 offenders dating back to 1958. None of the analyses found that imprisoning people stopped them committing more crimes when they came out. If there is a change in the rate at which people leaving prison are convicted of another crime the first question that criminologists would ask is 'how have they changed their intake?', not 'what are they doing right?' Research shows that the best predictor of whether a convicted person will be reconvicted is past criminal record, number of previous prison sentences and social background.[50]

No-one who has read this far can be surprised at this finding. Those being punished come from the most marginalized groups in society. Their experience of prison is often brutal and usually negative. When they leave prison the outside world is unwelcoming if not hostile. Even the results of non-prison punishments are not very good in keeping convicted people away from further crime.

Secondly, it is hard to argue that the criminal justice system is what really controls and prevents crime when it actually touches very few of the crimes committed. Of all the crimes committed, only a small proportion is reported to the police. The police will find a suspect for an even smaller percentage of these reported crimes. Not all of these suspects will be convicted and punished, because sometimes the police get the wrong person and sometimes the evidence cannot be found. So, however good the system is, it will only ever be dealing with a small proportion of the crime in any society, although the more serious a crime is, the more likely it is to be investigated and punished.

Figures from England show that of 100 crimes that are estimated to be committed, 50 are reported to the police, 30 are recorded by the police as crimes, eight perpetrators are found, and one is convicted.[51]

United Nations surveys look at how many of the crimes of robbery reported to the police result in someone being convicted. In South-East Asia and the Pacific one out of every 35 cases reported led to a conviction.[52] The figure for Latin America and the Caribbean was one out of 15. Both North America and Western Europe showed a figure of one in nine.[53]

So the criminal justice system affects a small proportion of the crime committed and, as we have shown, puts an emphasis on the crimes of the poor. There is another argument often used to assert its effectiveness. Perhaps the criminal justice system controls crime *just by its existence*, because it is such a deterrent to people who might be thinking of committing a crime but decide against it because they might be caught and punished. Certainly this must be true in part. If there were no punishment system, more people would break the law. But its effect should not be exaggerated. It may deter those with a stake in society and a lot to lose from being convicted. For many others it is not a deterrent. They have little to lose. Furthermore, most people think they will not be caught, a reasonable assumption. Many, if they are drunk or enraged, do not think about the consequences before they commit a crime. Many will come from environments where crime is the way of life and the chance of being caught and punished is a risk that everyone accepts.

So how is it that such a belief has grown up that prison works and a lot of imprisonment is good value for money? In most countries, when politicians say they will build new prisons there is little protest. Such a decision is usually welcomed by Parliament and the public and the cost is not regretted. Between 1987 and 1998 spending on punishment in the United States increased by 30 per cent and spending on higher education decreased by 18 per cent.[54] Why has it been so easy to persuade the public that more imprisonment is a good path to follow?

Table 2.4

Changes in imprisonment rates and recorded crime rates for selected states, 1991–2001

State	Crime rate	Prison rate
Canada	−17%	+2%
Denmark	−9%	−9%
England and Wales	−11%	+45%
The Netherlands	+13%	+105%
Spain	+3%	+28%

Source: Gordon Barclay and Cynthia Tavares, *International Comparisons of Criminal Justice Statistics, 2001*, London: Home Office, 2003.

Many reasons are put forward. One is that prisons reduce crime. If the bad people are locked up crime will obviously fall. Those using this argument point to the fall in the crime rate in the United States and the rapid rise in its prison population. Between 1990 and 2000 the US prison population rose by 68 per cent. Its crime rate fell by 20 per cent. So the claim is made that the fall in crime is a result of locking up lots of criminals. But it is not so easy to show that the one leads to the other.

So it is hard to argue that there is a simple relationship between crime rates and the number of people in prison. Obviously there is some relationship. Some analysts have estimated that 15 per cent of the reduction in the US crime rate is due to locking up so many young men from poor areas.[55] Research in England has suggested that increasing the prison population there by 25 per cent might reduce the crime rate by 1 per cent. However the evidence does not support the idea that keeping large numbers of people in prison reduces the level of crime and that mass imprisonment makes society safer. Perhaps the clearest answer comes from looking at the differences between two countries in North America, the US and Canada (Table 2.5).

These two countries are similar in many ways. Where they differ is in their approach to social policy.

Table 2.5
Prison population rates, homicide rates and crime rate changes compared, US and Canada

	US	Canada
Prison population rate per 100,000 (2003)	715	116
Homicide rate per 100,000 (average of 1999–2001)	5.56	1.77
Changes in crime rate (1991–2001)	−2.0%	−1.8%

Source: Gordon Barclay and Cynthia Tavares, *International Comparisons of Criminal Justice Statistics, 2001*, London: Home Office, 2003.

There are as many theories about the causes of crime and violence as there are attitudes to life. Everyone will have a view. It is the programmes on the television. It is the break-up of the family. The lack of discipline in schools must be to blame. There are no jobs for young people; that is the reason. The decline of religion must be to blame. Poverty, alcohol and drugs, breakdown of authority, computer games, mothers going out to work, single parenthood are all suggested.

Perhaps it is better to ask what can protect us from crime. Human security and protection from crime come from social cohesion. 'At the community level, cohesion is an asset that provides security [and] regulates behaviour.'[56] People are less likely to prey on each other and steal from each other when they live in an environment where they are known, have a sense of belonging, are respected, have a sense of obligation to those around them and would suffer from a strong sense of shame if they were caught out in wrongdoing, because the opinion of those amongst whom they live matters to them. Social spending on health and education create an environment where violent crime is less likely to flourish.

In New Zealand the prison population increased by 50 per cent between 1995 and 2004. Justice Minister Phil Goff told the New Zealand people in 2004, as he launched forecasts of yet more prisoners in the years to come,

> The projected increase in the prison population is not the result of increasing crime…. Tougher sentencing comes at a high cost…. It's money we'd much rather spend on areas like health and education…. Over the longer term, it will be measures to address the causes of crime, rather than simply prisons, which will bring down crime.[57]

The UN's Global Action Plan on Human Settlements called in 1996 for cities to take crime prevention measures that addressed the 'underlying factors which undermine community safety … such as poverty, inequality, family stress, unemployment, absence of educational and vocational opportunities, and lack of health care'.[58]

This chapter has tried to show that crime is often a matter of definition, that there is potential in any society for defining more acts as crimes, or going instead for a smaller criminal justice system and correspondingly more expenditure on social welfare. It has also suggested that a safer and more equal society is likely to prefer to minimize criminal justice and maximize social justice. In the next chapter we look at some trends and show how the opening up of criminal justice systems to market forces is driving some countries in the opposite direction.

Notes

1   Nils Christie, *A Suitable Amount of Crime*, London: Routledge, 2002, pp. ix–x.
2   See *The Children Act 2004*, Chapter 31, London: HMSO, 2004.
3   Mark Tully, 'Ram Chander's Story', in *No Full Stops in India*, Harmondsworth: Viking, 1991, p. 38.
4   Audrey Gillan, 'Woman "Brought to Senses" Now Supports Jail as a Way to Tackle Bad Parenting', *Guardian*, 27 May 2002.
5   Nick Cohen, '661 New Crimes – and Counting', *New Statesman*, 7 July 2003.

6   Gene Healy, *Go Directly to Jail: the Criminalization of Almost Everything*, Washington DC: Cato Institute, 2004, p. xi.

7   *Ibid.*, pp. viii–ix.

8   United Nations Children's Fund, *Old Enough to Be a Criminal? Special Protections Progress and Disparity*, 1997.

9   *V v The United Kingdom,* ECHR, Application no. 24888/94, 16 December 1999.

10 'Young Killers Shown Compassion', BBC News, 30 June 2000.

11 Nils Christie, *A Suitable Amount of Crime*, p. 7.

12 'Nepal Pardon for Women Prisoners', BBC News, 11 August 2004.

13 'Nigeria: Amina Lawal Is Free at Last', in *The Wire* (Amnesty International magazine), November 2003.

14 'Mentally Ill Man Executed in US', BBC News, 7 January 2004.

15 See Mark Shaw, Jan van Dijk and Wolfgang Rhomberg, 'Determining Trends in Global Crime and Justice: an Overview of Results from the United Nations Surveys of Crime Trends and Operations of Criminal Justice Systems', in *Forum on Crime and Society*, 3, 1–2 (December 2003), United Nations Office on Drugs and Crime, Vienna.

16 Cited in World Health Organization, *Summary: World Report on Violence and Health*, Geneva: WHO, 2002, p. 15.

17 Haydee Marin and Fatima Seife, *Law and Status of Peruvian Women*, Germany: International Society for Human Rights, 2003.

18 Penal Reform International, *An Interview with Yury Ivanovich Kalinin, Russian Deputy Justice Minister*, London, October 1998.

19 See John van Kesteren, Pat Mayhew and Paul Nieuwbeerta, *Criminal Victimisation in Seventeen Industrialised Countries: Key Findings from the 2000 International Crime Victim Survey*, The Hague: Wetenschappelijk Onderzoeks- en Documentatiecentrum (WODC), 2001, pp. 17–18.

20 *Ibid.*, p. 25.

21 *Ibid.*, p. 26.

22 *Ibid.*, p. 27.

23 *Ibid.*, p. 29.

24 *Ibid.*, p. 33.

25 *Ibid.*, p. 40.

26 *Ibid.*, p. 45.

27 Mark Shaw, Jan van Dijk, and Wolfgang Rhomberg, 'Determining Trends', pp. 44–5.

28 Gordon Barclay and Cynthia Tavares, *International Comparisons of Criminal Justice Statistics, 2001*, London: Home Office, 2003.

29 Richard J. Evans, *Rituals of Retribution: Capital Punishment in Germany, 1600–1987*, Harmondsworth: 1997, p. 250.

30 *Ibid.*, p. 254.

31 'Section 1, Crime and Punishment in the US', based on data for 2001, in *The Prison Index* <www.prisonpolicy.org>.

32 Quoted in Department for International Development, *Justice and Poverty Reduction*, London, 2000, p. 3.

33 Deepa Narayan *et al.*, *Voices of the Poor: Can Anyone Hear Us?* New York: Oxford University Press for the World Bank, 2000, p. 251.

34 See United Nations Development Programme, *Human Security in Bangladesh: in Search of Justice and Dignity*, UNDP, 2002.

35 Associated Press, 'Mexico Sacks Entire Police', 13 April 2004.

36 *Criminal Justice Newsletter*, Washington DC: Pace Publications, 17 February 2004, p. 3.

37 Deepa Narayan *et al.*, *Voices of the Poor*, p. 251.

38 *Ibid.*, p. 234.

39 Noel Sichalwe, 'LAZ Welcomes Suspension of Two Magistrates over Corruption', *The Post*, Lusaka, 12 April 2004.

40 'Top Bangladesh Judge Sacked', BBC News, 20 April 2004.

41 Tony Kago and Jillo Kadida, 'Revealed: Top Judges Caught in Corruption', *Daily Nation*, 1 October 2003.

42 National Legal Aid and Defender Association, *An Assessment of Trial-Level Indigent Defence Services in Louisiana 40 years after Gideon*, March 2004, p. iii.

43 The Sentencing Project, *Crack Cocaine Sentencing Policy: Unjustified and Unreasonable*, Washington DC, 1997.

44 From *The Bush Administration Takes Aim: Civil Rights Under Attack*, the Leadership Conference on Civil Rights, April 2003, www.civil-rights.org.

45 Tushar Kansal and Marc Mauer, *Racial Disparity in Sentencing: a Review of the Literature*, Washington DC: The Sentencing Project, 2005, p. 1.

46 *Ibid.*, p. 2.

47 *Ibid.*, p. 15.

48 Amnesty International, *Singapore, the Death Penalty: a Hidden Toll of Executions*, 2004.

49 *Prison Statistics, England and Wales 2002*, London: Home Office, 2003.

50 See International Centre for Prison Studies, 'Analysis of International Policy and Practice on Reducing Reoffending by Ex-Prisoners, Report for the Social Exclusion Unit', London, 2001 (unpublished).

51 See *Digest 4: Information on the Criminal Justice System in England and Wales*, London: Home Office, 1999.

52 See Mark Shaw, Jan van Dijk and Wolfgang Rhomberg, 'Determining Trends', p. 52.

53 *Ibid.*, p. 53.

54 Tara-Jen Ambrosio and Vincent Schiraldi, *From Classrooms to Cellblocks:*

a National Perspective, Washington DC: Justice Policy Institute, 1999, p. 5.

55 See Alfred Blumstein (series editor) and Joel Wallman (editor), *The Crime Drop in America,* Cambridge: Cambridge University Press, 2000 (new edition).

56 Deepa Narayan *et al., Voices of the Poor,* p. 220.

57 Address at the launch of the Ministry of Justice's Annual Update of Forecasts of the Prison Population, Department of Justice, New Zealand, 2004.

58 United Nations, *Habitat Agenda Section IVc, Sustainable Human Settlements Development in an Urbanizing World,* 7 August 1996.

3

Crime – a Good Business?
The Impact of the Free Market

3 prison stocks poised to break out

Thanks in part to overcrowding, governments are turning to private companies to build and manage prisons. Here's how to pick the right time to buy into the trend.

In what might be a revealing commentary on our country's state of affairs, the nation's private prison companies look like solid investments for the next several years.

The three big prison companies – Corrections Corporation of America … the Geo Group … and even the troubled Cornell Companies … have decent growth prospects….

Michael Brush, 'Company Focus'[1]

In Chapter 1 we caught a glimpse of the prisons of the world and saw how little they can contribute to rehabilitation and how much misery, disease and brutality they inflict on those who live and work in them. We saw that they contain not a cross-section of the population of any country, but a concentration of the disadvantaged, the marginalized and those facing race and other discrimination. We saw how vulnerable children, women and mentally ill people are imprisoned, and what imprisonment does to them.

In Chapter 2 we looked at how acts become defined as crimes and how these crimes are then policed and punished. The chapter aimed to show how, in defining and dealing with crime, a bias exists that explains why the prisons are disproportionately peopled with the poor and the powerless. At all points in the criminal justice process the poor face the most difficulties and the least chance of a just outcome. Chapter 2 also showed the limitations of the criminal justice system and of punishment in containing crime, and the importance of wider social policy measures for safety and human security.

Chapters 1 and 2 show that the system that operates in most countries is inequitable and damaging, and does not fulfil its aims. This chapter describes trends and developments in the globalizing world economy that are compounding the injustice. If these trends are allowed to continue and take hold worldwide, they will create a bright future for the private market in crime control but a frightening future for much of humanity.

First it is important to try to unravel the connections between what is happening in the global economy and the levels of crime and violence in people's everyday lives. Is there a connection? What has been the impact of the 'greater reliance on market forces in economic development'[2] and 'the Washington Consensus policies that the international financial institutions have imposed'?[3] Former World Bank economist Joseph Stiglitz saw much harm coming out of the imposition of these policies. 'For millions of people', he wrote, 'globalization has not worked.' People are worse off because their jobs have been destroyed and their lives have become 'more insecure'. They have been overcome by feelings of powerlessness in the face of 'forces beyond their control'. They have 'seen their democracies undermined, their cultures eroded'.[4]

We look first at the impact of these changes on crime and violence. How true is it that the spread of the global marketplace has led to a breakdown in those aspects of a society that hold it together and keep people from preying on each other, seizing property and resorting to violence? Secondly, we review the entry of the market into the provision of security, policing and prisons, and the commercialization of these state functions.

More Free Markets – More Crime?

What has been the effect on the many millions of people for whom, as Joseph Stiglitz says, 'globalization has not worked'? Is living with crime and insecurity another burden placed on them by these processes?

The parents of a young South African called Herschel Schop bear such a burden. They live in Cape Town. Their son Herschel, aged fifteen, was found murdered on the morning of 27 January 2005 by a passer-by. Apparently he had been hit on the head and stabbed in the back. When he was found he was barefoot. His red Nike trainers were missing.[5] In 1989 another 15-year-old, Michael Thomas, was found strangled in the woods near his school in Maryland, United States. He too was found barefoot. His two-weeks-old basketball shoes were taken. In Chicago, a 19-year-old was shot for the jacket he was wearing.[6] In Buenos Aires, a criminologist described young criminals and 'the aggressive behaviour they engage in to steal a pair of tennis shoes or a wallet. By contrast with previous years, today they use arms, hurt their victims, kill them.'[7]

Young people killing other young people for their shoes, their jackets, their electronic gadgets is a twenty-first-century phenomenon. It seems to symbolize how violence, crime and the consumerism of a market society come together in one terrible conjunction. How did so many young men get to this point? Why is it a feature of urban life in so many different places?

In this chapter we try to show the pathway that leads to such acts. We saw in Chapter 2 how social cohesion is a great bulwark against personal and community crime. There is normally less crime when people live in small communities, know their neighbours and are known, when children are seen as everyone's responsibility, when strong policies to promote social inclusion are in place and trust is widespread. How far can the changes to that way of life since the late 1970s be shown to lead to increased levels of violence, crime and corruption? This is not an easy question to answer and a number of forces are at work. However, many have argued that there is a clear connection.

One of those making the case is the leading US criminologist Elliott Currie. He writes about the forces at work in American society that have reduced the capacity of some communities to deal with crime. In his work he distinguishes between a 'market economy' and a 'market society'. A market economy is one where there is a balance between public and private provision. A market society is one in which

> the pursuit of private gain increasingly becomes the organising principle for all areas of social life, not simply a mechanism which we use to accomplish certain circumscribed ends. The balance between private and public shifts dramatically, so that the public retreats to a miniscule and disempowered part of social and economic life and the idea of common purposes and common responsibility withers as an important social value.

Such societies are, he notes, 'extraordinarily fertile ground for the growth of crime'.[8] And he concludes that 'The growth of market society is a multi-faceted process which is at its core destructive of the economic, social and cultural requisites of social peace and personal security.'[9]

The World Bank study of the experiences of the poor in facing up to the threats to their security in everyday life has already been discussed in Chapter 2. That report, *Voices of the Poor*, analysed the process through which economic difficulties and increased poverty lead gradually to increased crime. By tracing the experiences of poor people as they encounter crime and insecurity, we can mark the route from relative social peace to widespread social mayhem.

The first step on that path is living a life constantly undermined by a shortage of money. Many people are getting poorer. For example, in 13 of the 18 Latin American countries the minimum wage in 1998 was lower than it had been in 1980, two decades before.[10] Since 1991 many living in countries that were formerly part of the Soviet Union have fallen into deep poverty.

Living in poverty is very stressful and leads to conflict and violence. A woman in Latvia reported that the atmosphere at home made her sons 'aggressive, ready to fight'.[11] In Ethiopia poor people said that unemployment leads to 'behaviour and acts which are morally unacceptable'.[12] This view of the effects of being poor on the way people behave to each other has been supported by others. Peter Screen, Archbishop of Kumasi, told a congress of Catholic prison chaplains in 2003: '[F]or Africa, I would like to place poverty at the hub of the causes of criminality. Poverty in Africa can be abject and dehumanizing. It is often such that it makes young men and women desperate.'[13]

A human rights group in Uganda, the Foundation for Human Rights Initiative, reports that poverty makes people more likely to take the law into their own hands. 'On many occasions', according to their human rights report, 'suspects, or criminals for that matter, are killed for committing petty crimes like stealing a chicken, a bunch of *matooke*, or a goat .... Such crimes may be termed petty, but to the public, they are not.' This, the report confirmed, was mainly due to the persistent problem of poverty in many communities; 'people have become very intolerant to crimes like theft because of the trouble and difficulties they face in trying to provide for their families and homes'.[14]

Poverty is often blamed for crime. The connection, though, is not that simple. Poor communities are not necessarily crime-ridden communities. Poverty does not always drive people to rob their neighbours, to steal crops from fields, to kill each other. Often poor communities are self-supporting, with a strong sense of shared values, an informal structure for helping each other with life's ups and downs, and many traditions that bind the community together. It is when life is disrupted and the bonds that keep people together are fractured that crime and insecurity take over.

In such fractured communities people turn against each other. The young see no reason to respect adults. Adults lose confidence in their capacity to discipline the young. Restraints based on reciprocal relationships break down. There are no respected community leaders left to reinforce norms and standards. The balance between the norms of the group and the outside pressures shifts and lawlessness becomes more acceptable.[15] People in Ukraine reported in 1996 that seedlings planted in the ground were stolen overnight.[16] People see that 'new opportunities are limited to the rich, the powerful, or the criminal'. Instead of mutual respect and reliance, mistrust grows between neighbours and they begin to fear each other. Levels of interpersonal violence rise.

In the United States and many other countries, lack of secure jobs and the growth of inadequate jobs mean working long hours with sub-standard child care. Many single parents have little time to spend on bringing up children; two parents often hold down four jobs between them and barely meet, even at weekends. In such circumstances young children are reared by default by older children on the street. They soon begin to see the street gang as a more important reference point than the family and the rules of the gang as the rules of life.

When poverty increases, people are faced with stark choices. If they are to survive, they may have to go away and seek work elsewhere, leaving home and their families behind. This destroys the structure and cohesion of neighbourhoods, villages and even whole states.[17]

People move around much more to find employment. So, 'market society promotes crime by weakening the capacity of local communities for "informal" support, mutual provision and socialization and supervision of the young'.[18] Low-cost housing is harder to get. People are less attached to an area and have less time to put into activities that are not about day-to-day survival. Communities that in the past helped people to cope and created a structure in which the young were socialized are destroyed.

Services that once served as a safety net and were widely available shrink and become more subject to strict tests and rationing. Cuts in welfare provision have been a feature of many Western European and former Soviet countries. Bob Deacon, in his *Globalization and Social Policy: the Threat to Equitable Welfare*, notes that 'Globalization sets welfare states in competition with each other', which 'generates the danger of ... a race to the bottom in terms of welfare provisioning'.[19]

Inequality grows. Some people become very rich and can buy more of everything than they could ever need or want. The purpose of life is explained as being able to buy more things, better things, more expensive things. Policies in the United States have created a huge gap between good, well-paid jobs at the top and insecure, poverty-wage jobs at the bottom. At the same time the welfare payments available to the poorly paid and the unemployed have shrunk. The result, according to Elliot Currie, has raised 'the top to unprecedented pinnacles of wealth and of personal consumption, while dropping the poor into a far deeper and more abysmal hole'.[20]

A 2004 report by the International Labour Organization notes that incomes in the United Kingdom and the United States became more unequal between the mid-1980s and the mid-1990s.[21] Even more striking has been the sharp increase in the share of the top 1 per cent of income earners in the US, the UK and Canada. A December 2003 report from the London School of Economics notes that in the UK 'there has been a growth in lousy jobs ... together with a growth in lovely jobs ... and a decline in the number of middling jobs'.[22]

Two things happen as a result of these changes. Sometimes the crime that has sprung up in the countryside, the towns and the cities penetrates the political and social system itself. Power moves to illegal groupings and mafia. At the level of the whole society, corruption spreads and it 'erodes the trust that a society needs to function effectively. Corruption makes equal access and fair treatment from the state impossible for the poor and excluded.... Corruption is a central reason why societies grow more insecure.'[23]

What also happens is that, in the neighbourhoods where informal social control has been destroyed and families are struggling to survive economically, another set of values takes over. Entertainments urging consumption of high-status items and emphasizing violence are beamed into every home. This is the road societies travel down to reach the point where Herschel Schop and Michael Thomas can be murdered for their training shoes.

More Free Markets – More Violence?

The growth of violence in many parts of the world is unarguable. Armenians reported in 1996 that violence had become so pervasive that 'the streets have invaded the classroom'. Moldovans reported in 1997 that brutal attacks on both men and women were common because police protection was no longer available.[24] Two sociologists from Latin America, Roberto Briceño-Leon and Verónica Zubillaga, write about violence and globalization in their region. Their focus is the huge growth in violence in Latin America and the Caribbean in the 1980s and 1990s. By 1998, they note, 'violence was the leading cause of death among people in the 15–44 age group'.[25]

What explains the increase in violence and the high levels it has reached in some countries? Three economists set out to establish whether there was a link between inequality and violent crime. Could a growth in levels of violence be attributed to a huge gap between rich and poor? They studied the subject from all aspects, eliminated all other possible explanations and came up with a clear conclusion: '[I]ncome inequality, measured by the Gini index[26] has a significant and positive effect on the incidence of crime.' The crimes measured were murder and robbery, and the results apply using different countries, different time periods and different measures of inequality of incomes.[27] Similar work was carried out by a criminologist from Rotterdam. He found that rates, not just of murder and other violent crimes, but also of theft and damage to cars, were higher in countries with high levels of income inequality.[28]

Joseph Stiglitz also sees a connection between inequality and crime. 'America has one of the largest proportions of its population behind prison bars and part of the reason is surely the huge inequalities in its society.'[29] The World Health Organization, in its study of *Small Arms and Global Health*, lists 'poverty and in particular inequalities within societies'[30] as an underlying cause of the growth in violence.

So, one cause of high rates of crime and violence is the high level of inequality now found in many societies. The illicit drugs trade is another, to be discussed in more detail in the next chapter. A third is the spread of firearms. Training shoes are not the only status symbol for young men displaced from their roots and seeking an identity. Guns can be very attractive. The spread of lethal weapons is widespread. In northern Kenya the pastoral Pokot people used to protect their herds of animals with spears. Now they have automatic rifles that have reached them from neighbouring war zones. In 2001 the young men went to a nearby community on a cattle raid. It turned out very badly. They killed 47 people with their weapons. One young man told a journalist, 'If you don't have a weapon, your grave is open.'[31]

Gun possession is a very serious problem in South Africa. Estimates vary but there may be four million guns in civilian hands.[32] In 2000, figures showed that murder, usually with a firearm, was the leading cause of death of young men aged between 15 and 21.[33]

In Brazil in the year 2000 more than 45,000 people were murdered. In poor urban areas and for the age group of young men, the murder rate is 230 per 100,000. In Rio de Janeiro between 1991 and 1999 there were more deaths caused by firearms than there were in the same period in Sierra Leone, even though conflict raged in Sierra Leone at that time. Between 1998 and 2000 there were more such deaths in Rio de Janeiro than in war-torn Yugoslavia.[34]

According to the World Bank study:

> Around the world social fragmentation is associated with major economic disruptions and frustration that new opportunities are limited to the rich, the powerful, or the criminal: migration in search of employment; and an overall environment of lawlessness, crime and violence combined with failure of systems of police and justice.[35]

Trends in the Use of Prison

Whether crime is rising or falling, what is going up everywhere are numbers of prisoners. The prison populations of the world are growing. Between November 1998 and June 2004 the known prison population increased by one million, from 8.1 million to 9.1 million. Not all countries are involved in this increase. There are 173 countries where the information is good enough to monitor changes in the prison population over time. In a three-, four- or five-year period the prison population has risen in two-thirds of these countries. In the other third, it has either gone down or remained stable. It has risen in just under two-thirds of African countries, just over two-thirds of countries in the Americas, 87 per cent of Asian countries, two-thirds of European countries and half of the countries in Oceania.[36]

Saudi Arabia and Singapore have tripled their numbers of prisoners since 1992. Another country showing a very substantial increase is Brazil where the increase between 1993 and 2003 was 144 per cent. The number of prisoners in Haiti, where prison conditions have long been life-threatening and where in 2003 three-quarters of the prisoners did not have a bed,[37] has increased by one and a half times over the period. Thailand since 1992 has seen a near-doubling of its prison population, as has Indonesia since 1993.

Table 3.1

Countries showing increases of more than 50 per cent in their prison populations between 1992 (or 1993) and 2004

Andorra	Cyprus	Netherlands
Argentina	El Salvador	Nicaragua
Australia	Ghana	Panama
Bahrain	Guatemala	Peru
Bangladesh	Haiti	Philippines
Barbados	Honduras	Saudi Arabia
Belarus	Indonesia	Serbia and Montenegro
Belize	Iran	Singapore
Bolivia	Ireland	Spain
Bosnia Herzegovina	Japan	Sri Lanka
Brazil	Kyrgyzstan	Thailand
Burundi	Macedonia	Turkey
Cambodia	Malawi	Ukraine
Chile	Malaysia	UK (England and
Columbia	Malta	Wales)
Costa Rica	Mexico	Uruguay
Croatia	Morocco	USA

Source: *World Prison Brief*, January 2005.

Turkey, Bahrain, Cyprus, Nicaragua, Honduras, Croatia and Kyrgyzstan have doubled their number of prisoners since 1992. The Netherlands, Costa Rica, Cambodia and Panama have seen an increase of over 140 per cent since 1992. In the United States the number of prisoners has increased from 501,000[38] in 1980 to just over two and a quarter million in the middle of 2004.[39]

The Market in Imprisonment

These increases in the number of prisoners have not gone unnoticed by those interested in the business potential of incarceration. When privatization of state companies and assets spread across the world in the 1970s and 1980s it was inevitable that privatizing prisons would be on the agenda. If water supplies, gas, electricity, telecoms and railways could be privatized, then private companies coming in and locking people up on behalf of the state would surely not be a bad idea, either. Prisons are a big state business, often staffed by unionized workers who wield a lot of power. Private prisons could probably bring more efficiency, that is efficiency defined as the same service for a lower cost, and get governments a better deal. Instead of having to find the money to build a prison, why not get a private company to raise the money, build the prison and then just charge the state an agreed rent for each bed used by a prisoner each night? Such a system would spread the cost of constructing the building over many years and the taxpayers and voters would be less likely to notice how much was being spent on imprisonment, or argue about whether a new prison was a good use of money.

These seem to be attractive arguments. Perhaps surprisingly, though, private prison companies did not enjoy a rapid or trouble-free penetration of the market. The first recent[40] experiment in handing over incarcerated adults to a private company to look after was conducted in the United States in 1979 when Ronald Reagan was President and Ed Meese was Attorney-General. Two centres for those detained by the US Immigration and Naturalization Services were privatized, in Houston and Laredo in Texas.[41]

By 1988, nine years after the two privatized immigration detention centres opened, only one in every hundred of US prison places was in private hands. Development was very slow until President Reagan set up a commission, the President's Commission on Privatization (1988), which recommended the use of private companies to run prisons in the US.[42] Twenty years of hard work and lobbying have been needed to get the private companies to the position they hold in 2005, when they have a foothold in a few countries and have been ignored by many others. In the United States in 2004, 6.6 per cent of all prisoners were held in private prisons,[43] up from 6.5 per cent in 2003.[44] Private prisons are to be found in 34 of the 50 US states and in the Federal Bureau of Prisons,[45] which is run by the federal government and holds those prisoners sentenced under federal rather than state laws. Private prisons in the US are concentrated in states in the South and the West, with the greatest number in Texas.[46]

In the United Kingdom, described by one of the private companies as 'the second largest private correctional market in the world',[47] and by another as 'the most privatised criminal justice system in Europe',[48] nine out of every hundred prisoners are in privately run prisons. Australia leads the world in privatizing, with nearly double that percentage. In South Africa, just over 3 per cent are held in two large private prisons, both maximum security. One, Kutama Sinthumulu prison, is in Louis Trichardt. The other, Mangugang, run by Global Solutions (formerly Group 4 Securitas), is in Bloemfontein.[49] New Zealand had one private prison, for pre-trial prisoners only, in Auckland – but the New Zealand government passed a law withdrawing the possibility of private prisons and closed its only private prison in July 2005.[50]

Different approaches have been taken to privatization, depending on the political environment of the country in question. In France there are no private prisons as such. However, 21 prisons out of the existing 185 and another six prisons coming on stream, although run by the state, contract out all services such as catering and cleaning to private companies. This French model is being followed in Belgium,[51] where there is one such prison, and in Chile, where ten are planned.

In the UK the private contractors are in charge of the prisons they run but the government places a Controller in each prison to monitor the performance and check how far the contractor meets the terms of the contract. If there are failures in meeting the contract the contractor has to pay the government a fine. The Controller also carries out various functions that, it is felt, should not be in the hands of a non-state agent – such as punishing prisoners for offences against discipline.

Table 3.2
Percentage of prisoners held in private prisons

Country	Date	Percentage
Australia (overall)	2003	17.8
New South Wales	2004	10.0
Queensland	2004	24.0
Victoria	2004	35.0
Western Australia	2004	26.0
South Africa	2004	3.2
United States	2004	6.6
UK (England and Wales)	2004	9.1
UK (Scotland)	2004	9.0

Sources: Lenny Roth, 'Privatization of Prisons', Background Paper No. 3/04, Parliament of New South Wales, and official government statistics of other countries.

Speculative Commercial Prison Building

However, in all these countries new private prisons have been contracted for by the state after the government has taken a decision that money is available, that it will be spent on a new prison, and that the private sector should be asked to make a bid to build and manage it. In the United States imprisonment as a business has been taken much further than this and much further than in any other country. Some writers talk of the 'prison industrial complex' to describe the rapid and varied growth in the crime control business in the US and 'the importance of private interests in criminal justice policy'.[52]

In the United States small towns with a failing economic base have invited companies in to build a prison by giving various financial incentives and then hoping that the new prison places will be filled. Once the prison is built, the contractor has to find a customer to buy the beds so that the prison can be staffed and the beds filled. If that can be achieved, some of the town's unemployed people will be back in work and the money will start coming back to the private prison operator.

Such a system can only work if there are buyers. Customers have to be found: prison establishments that are looking for places to put some of their prisoners. In most countries this is not an idea that makes sense. Governments do not go shopping for beds for their surplus prisoners. If there is a crisis of prison overcrowding or a fire in a prison that destroys the cell spaces, they open old army camps, commission a disused ship (as happened in England when an old troop ship was taken over and became Her Majesty's Prison *The Weare*),[53] or introduce a programme to reduce the number of prisoners by releasing some before the end of their sentences.

In the US, however, there are customers. Officials responsible for state prisons, who have an urgent need for more cells in which to put their prisoners, go out and buy what they need. This shopping is not restricted to their own state, however. They buy where they can find the prison beds, even when this means prisoners are far from their homes and families (distances up to 3,000 miles are possible) and out of touch with any social reintegration services in their home areas. The State of Wisconsin, for instance, placed 1,510 of its prisoners in a private prison called Whiteville run by the Corrections Corporation of America (CCA) in Tennessee. Some of them were involved in a disturbance there in 1999. Ten prisoners took fifteen members of staff hostage and 'chemical agents' were used to bring the incident to an end.[54] Wisconsin continued to shop for private prison places in other states until 2004. In 2001, 4,253 prisoners from Wisconsin were being imprisoned in other states: Tennessee, Texas, West Virginia, Oklahoma and Minnesota. But for Wisconsin this buying beds in faraway places was a temporary measure. New public prisons opened in Wisconsin and by May 2004 the number of farmed-out prisoners was down to 855.[55]

Wisconsin is but one example. Arizona became home to 557 prisoners from Hawaii sent to Florence Correctional Facility, 45 miles from Phoenix and 3,000 miles from home. The prison belonged to the Corrections Corporation of America and was completed in 2000. After the Hawaiian prisoners were moved in, in April 2001 a team from the Department of Public Safety in Hawaii made a monitoring visit to the Florence Correctional Facility to see how they were getting on. The team reported that the Hawaiian prisoners seemed not to have settled well. However, the female member of the visiting team did not join the inspection 'due to the hostile environment'. It was discovered that during April there had been six prisoner assaults and two prisoners had died. 'A riot occurred' involving prisoners and staff. One prisoner allegedly drank a bottle of cleaning fluid. The part of the prison where the prisoners lived was not visited 'due to the hostile environment'. The recreation area was not visited 'due to the hostile environment'. The medical unit was not visited 'due to the hostile environment'.[56]

The District of Columbia, containing America's capital, had been a prison-beds shopper for many years, sending prisoners far and wide. In 1988 a large group of prisoners from Washington DC were sent to Washington State, 2,720 miles away. They did not like being so far from home and behaved disruptively until the governor of the state asked that they be sent back. They were returned.

In the early 1990s some prisoners from the District of Columbia were sent to a private prison run by CCA in Mason, Tennessee. They were disruptive and force was used to bring them under control. Eventually they too were returned home because the money was not available to pay CCA to continue to keep them.[57]

Youngstown in Ohio became home to 1,700 sentenced prisoners from the District of Columbia – with serious consequences, as we shall see below. By building prisons as part of a plan for economic development in depressed areas, country towns have become home to a thousand or more people, usually from the cities, and many of the townspeople have become prison guards.

The Argument for Commercially Run Prisons

Many of the supporters of private sector prisons start from the premise that, as we have seen in Chapter 1, state-run prisons are often very bad places, inefficiently and inhumanely run, corrupt and violent. The prison staff exert too much power and refuse to bring in many reforms that would improve the prison and the treatment of prisoners. Prison staff, it is said, do not want prisoners to have access to education because they do not deserve it. They do not want prisoners to get to see the doctor because they are only malingering. They do not want prisoners to have access to protective methods such as condoms and clean needles because that would condone illegality. The prison staff are in trade unions that fight any moves to change working hours or working practices. They are more interested in getting paid well, having a secure pension and a quiet life than in running good prisons. The answer to those arguments is obvious, say the supporters of privatization. Bring in a private contractor; agree a contract; pay an agreed price and get a better and more flexible service, and lots of new ideas about how to run prisons better and make them more effective. The introduction of the private sector prisons will make the state prison staff realize that if they do not discover a new attitude their jobs may be sold off too. Now that the state has a choice the public prison employees are vulnerable. Their power is reduced and the fear of privatization will be a spur to them to do better, work harder, argue less and accept changes in working practices which cut public sector costs.

On the face of it, this is a difficult argument to fault. Many state-run prisons are indeed hell-holes of neglect and brutality. No private company, it is thought, could do worse, because with a private company there is a contract that has to be honoured and a business reputation that has to be maintained. If the contract is not honoured, it can be terminated. Reforming a bad state prison is much more difficult than ending a contract and choosing another contractor. Even in a rich country like England, where the public prisons are not too bad, if prisoners had a choice which prison would they prefer? Would they choose the prison painted grey and brown and infested with mice, with stained and ragged bedding and uniforms that do not fit, run by disgruntled state-employed prison officers, badly managed by a burnt-out official two years from retirement, in a building dating from the Napoleonic wars?[58]

They would probably prefer the private prison. This would be in a brand-new building painted in cheerful colours, perhaps with a fancy new name such as 'secure learning centre'. It would have state-of-the-art equipment. It would be staffed by smiling, recently trained, enthusiastic men and women wearing non-militaristic smart uniforms and working for a boss determined to do well because his or her performance bonus depends on it.

It has to be said that not all private sector prisons are bad prisons, by any means. However, the first limitation on the rosy picture of what privatization can bring, which has been noted by a number of commentators and researchers,[59] is that private prisons are not scandal-free or problem-free, either.

Private Sector Prisons – Some Experiences

One of the most controversial of private prison companies has been the Corrections Corporation of America, CCA. It was founded by Thomas Beasley, ex-chair of the Tennessee Republican Party, and was incorporated in Tennessee in 1983. It opened its first detention centre for immigrants in 1984.[60] One backer was an investor who formerly built up the Kentucky Fried Chicken chain and the Hospital Corporation of America, a private health care company which went on to pay $1.7 billion in fines for defrauding the federal government. Another associate was T. Don Hutto, a former prison administrator who had an interesting past. In 1978 the Supreme Court of the United States affirmed a ruling that the regime of the Arkansas Prison System constituted 'cruel and unusual punishment'. The case to the Supreme Court included allegations of rape and torture. At that time T. Don Hutto was in charge of the Arkansas Prison System. Also connected with CCA was Michael Quinlan, Head of the US Federal Bureau of Prisons from 1987 to 1992 and a man with many useful connections.

The history of CCA has been well documented. It is an eventful story and illustrates well the fortunes of private prisons more generally. The year 2000 was CCA's low point. It nearly went bankrupt. The Chief Executive, who was one of the founders, was forced to leave. Lawsuits totalling $120 million brought by unhappy investors had to be settled. There was an effort to make a new start and give a new impression. The pictures of the former Chief Executive, Doctor Crants, were removed from the corporate head office.

What was CCA trying to put behind it when these changes took place? The late 1980s and 1990s were difficult years for the company. Rosalyn Bradford was imprisoned in a CCA prison called Silverdale in Tennessee when she died from a complication arising from pregnancy. A lawsuit was brought against CCA in January 1988 alleging poor medical care and the company agreed to pay $100,000. In 1989 and 1990 a number of prisoners escaped from a new CCA prison in Florida. In December 1990 tear gas was used to put down a disturbance at the recently opened West Tennessee Detention Facility.[61] In 1993 the company was served with a federal civil rights lawsuit on behalf of three Puerto Rican prisoners who were shot during a disturbance at a detention centre in New Mexico.[62] In October 1995 more than one hundred prisoners in a CCA prison in West Tennessee rioted and caused a lot of damage. In August 1996 about 400 prisoners created a mass disturbance at a CCA federal detention centre in Texas.[63]

CCA won a $14 million contract with the State of South Carolina to operate a 400-bed training centre for young delinquents. Seven young people escaped in August 1996. Then it was found that staff members had been using excessive force on the young offenders. Another eight juveniles got away in February

1997. At this point the State of South Carolina decided not to renew the contract. Subsequently 'a federal jury awarded over $3 million in damages against the company and found that CCA had a policy and practice of mistreating youths at the facility'.[64] In May 1997 a disturbance at a CCA prison in Oklahoma left two guards injured.[65]

The most famous of CCA's problems was the Youngstown affair. The Youngstown area in the State of Ohio was once a flourishing industrial area based on steel mills. In its search for employment for the people laid off when the steel mills closed the town's leaders identified a big unused building that would make a good prison and tried to persuade the State of Ohio to use it for that purpose. Unfortunately for Youngstown a neighbouring area got the new state prison and the building stayed unused. But two new prisons, one state and one belonging to the federal government, were established in the area and the people of Youngstown discovered that prisons were 'friendly, economically viable projects'. But still the building lay empty. Eventually in 1995 the city offered the 103-acre site to CCA for one dollar, with the provision of access to water, sewerage, natural gas and electricity, and a three-year tax exemption. The company agreed to build a medium-security prison with 1,500 beds, to invest $35–40 million in building costs and to create around 350 full-time permanent jobs. After three years the annual wages bill was to reach $8 million. First preference in jobs would be given to residents of Youngstown, and CCA would aim to buy goods and services from businesses in the city. Finally, CCA agreed to give 50 prison cells to the city to use for its own prisoners at a reduced rate. This agreement was signed in March 1996. The prison opened in May 1997.

Who were the customers? Who bought the beds? The opening of the empty prison came at a very convenient time for another state prison system that was in trouble. The District of Columbia, containing Washington DC, was facing a crisis, not for the first time. For many years the Department of Corrections there had faced many challenges in court and much public scrutiny. A prison complex belonging to the District in a suburb of Virginia twenty miles south of Washington was suffering from poor conditions and inadequate accommodation. There had been many years of adverse publicity and campaigns to have the complex closed. CCA now had an empty prison and the District of Columbia was a likely customer. Two days after the interim contract was signed in May 1997 the prisoners began to be moved in.[66] From the beginning things did not go well. There were disturbances and stabbings. In July of that year an Ohio state legislator said. 'There is no doubt in my mind we have a bomb ticking in Youngstown.'[67]

In August 1997 a human rights lawyer filed a case on behalf of the prisoners, arguing that the prison was unsafe. By February 1998 there had been nineteen stabbings, two of which led to death. Derrick David was murdered on 22 February in a cell by two other prisoners, apparently in a quarrel about some personal property. Bryson Chisley was murdered in March in the most secure part of the prison by an enemy of his who managed to get out of handcuffs and stab him. After the two murders the staff instigated a lengthy search of all the housing units. According to the official report of the incident,

> Emergency teams heavily outfitted in riot gear ... led [the prisoners] shackled and naked out of their cells where they forced them to lie on the floor in groups or to kneel, leaning with their face against the wall for 30 or 60 minutes whilst the cells were searched.... [F]emale staff were present....

These procedures seemed 'intended to systematically degrade and humiliate' all the prisoners.[68]

Fifteen months after the prison opened, on 25 July 1998, six prisoners escaped in broad daylight. Four of them had been convicted of murder. They were eventually recaptured. A federal judge ordered the District of Columbia to stop sending its prisoners to Youngstown when he found that there was no proper security classification in operation and that prisoners from all sorts of back-grounds were being held together. The Mayor of Youngstown said, 'It's been a nightmare. [CCA's] credibility is zero.'[69] The prisoners took a lawsuit against the company because of their bad treatment, wholly inadequate medical care and lack of separation from other prisoners. The company eventually settled the case in 1999 for $1.65 million to the prisoners and $756,000 in legal fees.[70] The prison was shut down in July 2001: 500 staff lost their jobs.[71]

The events at Youngstown were so damaging to the concept of privatized prisons that when the free-market-oriented government of Ontario in Canada was considering privatization, an Ohio senator wrote to the Premier of Ontario Mike Harris to say 'Ohio's experi-ences with private prisons has been to date eventful yet wholly regrettable.'[72]

After the Youngstown affair the story of CCA continued in a more low-key way. By the year 2000 when the new management came in, business was not good. As many as 12,000 prison beds were up for sale but there were no buyers. Then salvation came in the shape of the Federal Bureau of Prisons. New policies after the events of 11 September 2001 led to a rapid increase in the number of federal prisoners and those detained under immigration powers. In 2005, in the town of Taylor in Texas, the T. Don Hutto Correctional Center run by CCA gained its accreditation with the Commission of Accreditation for Corrections. In June 2004 the prison had lost its contract with the local county and was preparing to close when the federal government stepped in and saved Taylor's prison.[73] Presumably none of those to be held in the new federal prison would know that it was named after the man who served as the Commissioner of Corrections in Arkansas from 1971 to 1976, a time when a District Court described the Arkansas system as 'a dark and evil world completely alien to the free world'.[74]

It is not just CCA that has problems. Wackenhut Corrections Corporation is a private security firm based in Florida that came into the incarceration market in 1984.[75] In 2000 the US Justice

Department sued the State of Louisiana and the Wackenhut Corrections Corporation over the treatment of all the young people held in the Jena Juvenile Justice Center in Louisiana. The Justice Department claimed that the young people were 'subjected to excessive abuse and neglect'.[76] The suit, which was to come up before a US District Court in Baton Rouge, alleged there was violence between the young people and by the staff on the young people, unreasonable use of isolation and restraints, and inadequate medical care. The department was asking the court to rule that the State of Louisiana should stop using 'corporal punishment, excessive force and gas grenades'. They should stop the staff putting prisoners in 'five-point restraints'. Five-point restraints are used to shackle a person to bed: to tie him or her to the bed by both arms, both legs and the waist. They should 'limit' the use of chemical restraints and isolation. They should stop punishing juveniles who harm themselves or try to commit suicide. In April 2000 the State of Louisiana took back management of the Jena Center.[77]

Other countries have had bad experiences too. In England Ashfield prison run by a company called Premier Prison Services got into great difficulties. Ashfield is a prison for young people under the age of 21. It could not fill its job vacancies and was operating with 11 per cent fewer staff than the contract specified. Two incidents of hostage taking and an incident where the prisoners refused to return to their cells from the exercise yard caused great concern. The Chief Inspector of Prisons in England said that her report on Ashfield was probably 'the most depressing I have issued in my time as Chief Inspector'.[78] In May 2002 for the first time the head of the prison service activated the law that allowed control to be taken back into the public sector. Ashfield was run for five months by the public prison service. Many of the prisoners were moved out. Then, in October 2002, the prison was given back to the company and they appointed a new director. Someone who had previously worked in the public prison service took the job.[79] In April 2003 it was still operating half full.[80] Another private prison, Parc, has been the subject of an inquiry by a governmental body, the Commission for Racial Equality, about allegations of racism by staff.[81] It also paid £859,000 altogether (about US$1.6 million) in fines for poor performance in its first two years.[82]

In October 2000, the government of the State of Victoria in Australia took back management of the Metropolitan Women's Correctional Centre near Melbourne from the Corrections Corporation of Australia, a joint venture company involving CCA. There had been three occasions when women were teargassed. On the last occasion one of the women was eight and a half months pregnant.[83]

The traffic from public to private sector has certainly not all been one-way. The State of North Carolina decided in 1997 to restrict building of new private prisons. They also took back under state control two prisons that were being run by the Corrections Corporation of America.[84] In England and Wales the contracts of two private prisons came up for renewal. The existing contractors applied to run the new contract and so did the public sector prison service. In 2001 the public sector prison service won the contracts.

Are Commercially Run Prisons Better?

Of course, not all private sector prisons are as dramatically scandalous as the above descriptions suggest. Many are peaceful, well-run establishments whose names never reach the columns of the commentators on the drawbacks of prison privatization. But when we consider the overall performance of private sector prisons and the contribution they make to improving the conditions of imprisonment and the treatment of prisoners – which as we saw in Chapter 1 are sorely in need of improvement – how well do they do? Is there evidence that private prisons are successful in terms of better prison policies?

Looking for evidence of the performance of private prisons compared with public prisons is a bit of a minefield. It is not easy to assess which sources are independent and which are connected to the industry or are part of the public relations machinery of an organization concerned about its share price. How can an ordinary person sort out which are objective? The story of Dr Charles Thomas illustrates the problem. Dr Charles Thomas is an expert on private prisons and was a professor at the University of Florida. He founded the Private Corrections Project and was often asked to comment on matters to do with private prisons. He produced many analyses of the private prison business and a lot of evidence that private prisons were better and cheaper.

Then the Florida Police Benevolent Association questioned Professor Thomas's appointment as a consultant to the Florida Correctional Privatization Commission because the private prison industry was part-financing his research. The Florida Police Benevolent Association complained about him to the Florida Commission on Ethics. In 1999 he was fined $20,000 by the Ethics Commission because he was found to be acting with a conflict of interest. He had received $3 million in consulting fees from a company linked to the Corrections Corporation of America. He also resigned from his post at the university.[85]

It is probably safer, therefore, to look to official sources for any evidence of relative performance and cost, though they are few. An important official report comparing the costs and quality of private and public prisons was produced by the US General Accounting Office (GAO) and presented to a committee of the US House of Representatives in 1996. The study reviewed five analyses comparing costs of private and public prisons and led the GAO to say: 'We could not conclude from these studies that privatization of correctional facilities will not save money. However, these studies do not offer substantial evidence that savings have occurred.'[86] One of the studies was of prisons in Tennessee. It found that the private prison cost per prisoner per day was $35.39. The two public prisons compared with it cost $34.90 and $35.45 respectively.[87]

A later report by the Bureau of Justice Assistance of the US National Council on Crime and Delinquency was published in 2001. The report studied private prisons in the United States and concluded that 'there are no data to support the contention that privately operated facilities offer cost savings over publicly managed facilities'. It also concluded that no 'definite research evidence' leads to the conclusion that services to prisoners and conditions of imprisonment are 'significantly improved in privately operated facilities'.[88] This report also compared matched samples of private and public prisons in the United States. It concluded that staffing in private prisons is 15 per cent lower, management information systems are less well organized and the number of major incidents is higher. Private prisons have a higher rate of assaults both of prisoners on other prisoners and prisoners against prison staff. The report concludes that 'private prisons operate much the same as public facilities.... No evidence was found to show that the existence of private prisons will have a dramatic effect on how non-private prisons operate.'[89]

A similar conclusion about rates of assaults was reached in a report produced in the United Kingdom. In June 2003 the National Audit Office, which scrutinizes public spending on behalf of the British Parliament, looked at the operational performance of private prisons. They found that relationships between staff and prisoners were better in private prisons but the rate of assaults was higher.[90] Staff turnover is higher in private prisons and main grade staff are paid less than people doing the same job in the public prisons. In private prisons there are fewer staff per prisoner than in public prisons.[91] In every aspect of working conditions, pay, pay range, overtime pay, pension arrangements and holidays allowed, the private prison main grade employees have a less good deal than the public prison officers.[92]

In their report they make three major points. First, the performance of private prisons in delivering what is in the contract 'has been mixed'.[93] Some private prisons have delivered and others have

not. Second, private prisons 'span the range of prison performance'.[94] The best are better than most of the public prisons. The
worst are at the bottom, amongst the least well-performing public
prisons. Third, private prisons have brought some innovation in the
use of technology and the way they recruit and use their employees,
but 'little difference in terms of the daily routine of prisons'. The
report concludes that the use of private prisons 'is neither a
guarantee of success nor the cause of inevitable failure'.[95]

The Opposition to Private Prisons

Considering the scale of privatization in other public sectors and the
efforts made to promote it throughout the world, privatization of
prisons has so far been modest. The study by the US Bureau of
Justice Assistance estimated that the whole private prison market
was worth about $1 billion in 1998.[96] One reason may be that it is a
high-risk business where the profit margins are not that impressive.
Another may be the strength of opposition that plans to privatize
prisons give rise to. Since privatization of incarceration was first
suggested it has seemed to many commentators and prison experts
to be a privatization too far.

The volume of writing and analysis about private prisons or in
opposition to private prisons has been large. Some commentators
have argued that it is simply unethical to make profit from locking
up human beings. Many have raised questions of accountability.
Taking away liberty has to be done within a framework of law and
human rights observance that is binding on states. Who will ensure
that the private contractors fulfill these obligations? Others have
argued from a more operational basis. Private companies are very
inexperienced, they say, and make many mistakes. They know they
have to make a profit, so the need to make a profit will take prece-
dence over the needs of the human beings in their care. When
something goes wrong the government has to pick up the pieces, as
the UK government had to do when Ashfield prison failed to

deliver a proper service. If a company goes out of business the government has to find a solution quickly.

The only achievement of private prisons, it is claimed, is to introduce competition so that workers in public prisons will reduce their wage demands and accept inferior working conditions out of fear of losing their jobs.

Does Privatization Influence the Direction of Penal Policy?

All the arguments noted above have been well aired and carry weight. The major fear, however, has been for the development of penal policy. Once there come into the field groups which make money out of imprisoning people, they will, quite understandably, want to promote and expand their business. So they will support policies which advocate a greater use of imprisonment and use their influence and access to government to support such policies. Aware of the strength of opposition to privatization of prisons, they may work in low-key ways to get their messages across. They may attend international conferences of justice officials and prison administrators, not to promote private prisons as such but to join in the conference generally. They may sponsor conferences that hard-pressed government bodies and non-governmental organizations want to run but cannot quite afford. More and more conference-goers will be running around with little shoulder bags advertising one of the private sector prison companies. In 2003 the groups that monitor the prisons in England and Wales and provide independent oversight, known as Independent Monitoring Boards, had sponsorship for their annual conference from the company Securicor.

The presence of private prison companies at such conferences and their participation in the professional meetings and interchanges between prison administrators changes the debate. It can lead to government officials being sucked into a world where prison expansion is assumed to be normal and desirable. The talk is of economies of scale and the latest technology, how to monitor prisoners by machines rather than by people. The private prison companies do not necessarily get business that day. They do not immediately call up the private jets so that public prison officials can be whisked away to see a state-of-the-art facility on another continent. But slowly these interactions can change the way the public sector prison directors see their work. The public sector people begin to talk about prisons as 'a business'. Their aim becomes to 'deliver a world-class product at lowest cost'. They forget they used to believe that prison should be used as a last resort. They forget that the prisons they run are full of many prisoners who should not be there. They may say to themselves, 'That's not my business. If the mood is expansionist, if everyone is in favour of more prisons, then I shall deliver what is wanted.'

Private prison companies in some countries also work hard at a political level to increase their business opportunities. In 1990 CCA's Chief Executive was quoted in the magazine *Business Week* as saying 'We literally spent millions of dollars educating our legislators on the advantages of private prison operators.'[97] The National Institute on Money in State Politics is an organization based in Montana in the United States that studies the role donations given to politicians play in the political process. The Institute found that during the 2000 elections in 14 Southern states, $1.1 million was given by private prison companies and their employees to 830 candidates.[98]

The influence of the companies is not just towards expansion of the prison business. They are also interested in reshaping imprisonment so that it is run in a business-like way and can yield a profit. The story of what happened in Lesotho is a good example. Lesotho is a country in Southern Africa with an annual GDP of $3,000 per head. In 2001 a remarkable paper was circulated to a range of people interested in prisons. It came from the Director of Prisons of Lesotho. He was asking for support for the Lesotho Prison Service's opposition to a new plan being considered by the government, the idea of bringing all the prisoners in Lesotho together from the four corners of the country and holding them in a new 3,500-bed private prison in Maseru. The paper says:

> A proposed private prison to be initiated and operationalized by 'Group Four' would pose a terrible threat to fundamental principles of Democracy, especially to a fledgling democracy like Lesotho. The danger of maintaining one big private prison which can house all inmates from around the country cannot be overemphasized. If this happens the notions of local government, decentralization of powers and prisons services, community participation in the correction of inmates and crime prevention are going to be in serious jeopardy.[99]

In the event, the proposal has not yet been accepted. It seems it is too expensive for Lesotho. The case of Lesotho illustrates the impact privatization could have on penal policy in a poor country. Lesotho would have set in stone a penal policy that required it for twenty years at least to find the money to pay for all 3,500 of its prisoners to be held, many of them far from their homes and families, in a prison run by a company based abroad, with its management abroad. The reintegration of prisoners would become more costly and more problematic because families would be unable to afford to visit. Should the government wish to change its penal policy, for example by keeping its prisoners near home in small open agricultural prisons or by introducing alternatives to prison, it could not be done, because for twenty years the money would have to go to the commercial prison company from another country to maintain the prison policy of the government of 2001.

The long-term effects of the private prison model are also being felt in South Africa. The Central prison in Maseru, Lesotho, is only 100 miles from Bloemfontein, home of one of South Africa's 3,000-bed private maximum security prisons. A warning about the high cost may well have come from South Africa. It seems that keeping its two private prisons running will absorb five per cent of the total revenue budget for the next 25 years. Yet these two prisons house only 3.2 per cent of South Africa's prisoners.[100]

So private prison companies tend to advocate economies of scale. One of the private prison companies noted in its magazine that 'South Africa is benefiting from economies of scale as home to the two largest private prisons in the world'.[101] There was no definition of the word 'benefiting'. They are also likely to favour employing technology rather than more human beings in their methods of dealing with prisoners. We have seen that private prisons operate with fewer staff than public prisons. They tend to replace staff with other methods of controlling prisoners. Other companies on the fringes of the private prison business sell a wide range of devices that can be used in imprisoning people, such as equipment that detects traces of illegal drugs on those visiting prisoners. The influence of private companies is likely to be towards a technological style of imprisonment rather than one based on human relationships.

Thus commercialization leads to the concentration of more prisoners in one place in order to achieve economies of scale and to a preference for technological methods of control rather than human interaction. The entry of private sector prison companies onto the criminal justice scene also strengthens and facilitates the continuation of the penal *status quo*. The increase in the growth of the number of prisoners in the world and the subsequent overcrowding can call forth two responses: more prisons or fewer prisoners. Chapters 1 and 2 have shown that there is no case for more prisons. There is a strong case for fewer prisoners. The argument in favour of more prisons is being made all the time by politicians and commentators. Those arguing against this approach face an uphill struggle. The presence in the debate of a well-funded business sector with an interest in more prisons and in perpetuating a way of dealing with prisoners that has not so far succeeded does not help the reform movement.

A single privately run prison – contracted out to the private sector but within a set of policies, laws, prisoners' rights, rehabilitation programmes and maintaining links with family and community

– is hardly objectionable. The private prison business is another matter. Building prisons as containment warehouses in some depressed area and then touting around the United States Departments of Corrections for persons to put in them, knocking a few cents off the daily rate to get the business, even if it means imprisoning Hawaiians in Arizona, is not imprisonment as it is understood in most parts of the world. Usually there is at least an ideology of social reintegration and laws that allow prisoners to retain some of their rights as citizens. But the private prison business is much more of a process of warehousing the unwanted, sending them into exile (a sort of Siberia), barely keeping them alive. You have to have a very different view of prisoners than that which is current in, say, France, Spain, South Korea or Chile – or that set out in the international norms and standards and accepted by the international community – to feel that such a policy can be put into practice.

Looking at the whole experience of privatizing prisons, some features emerge that are worthy of comment. Handing over the management of prisons to private sector providers and the creation of competition within the prison system have only taken hold in a very few English-speaking countries. In the United States privatization has been used mainly to deal with a crisis of shortage of prison places because of a sudden increase in the number of prisoners. In the UK and Australia it seems to have been used because those in charge of the prison systems there could not find another way to sort out historic bad management practices and failed staff relations. It is mainly designed to reduce the unit costs of a prison place and introduce fear as an element in the management of prison staff. It is not in any sense an experiment in prison reform.

Cashing in on Insecurity

As we have seen, the private prison business is very small. In spite of a wave of privatizations that has swept before it telecoms, airlines, water and electricity, only a minute proportion of the world's

9.1 million prisoners are in private prisons. The expansion of privately run prisons is sporadic and uneven. The companies gain new customers but lose others. The real private market is not in prisons as such, but in all of the fruits of fear. As we have shown, the spread of the free market leads to an increase in fear and insecurity. Some commentators have described a new politics of fear where politicians concentrate on crime, promise more measures to deal with it, and respond to legitimate public concern about particular crimes not with reassurance and preventive measures, but with heavier punishments and reduced protection for defendants.

In 1993 the Norwegian criminologist Nils Christie produced an important book, *Crime Control as Industry*, which set out the argument that, following the end of the Cold War, former military contractors looking for fresh business were entering the field of criminal justice, seeing a role for themselves in the 'war on crime' and adapting many of their products to the control of civilian populations. In Chapter 2 we made reference to another of his books, *A Suitable Amount of Crime,* published in 2004. In it he looks afresh at the way criminal policies are developed and at one point he writes, 'Our destiny in modern society is to live among strangers. This is a situation particularly well suited for giving unwanted acts the meaning of being crimes.'[102]

Strangers are by definition mysterious. We do not know who they are or what they might do. The risk society[103] is full of risky people. Governments try to convince the public that 'risky people' will be dealt with and there will be protection. Just as more unwanted acts become defined as 'crimes' so more unwanted people or needy people become 'risky' people. 'One of the strongest arguments for outsourcing justice services is the technological innovations that private suppliers can provide.' So wrote one of the private security companies, which claims to be the world's third-largest provider of electronic monitoring of human beings.[104] Huge computer systems with criminal records on them are developed. Software that is used by social workers and probation officers to assess risk is developed and sold. Putting electronic devices on people to control their movements is piloted and marketed. New ideas such as satellite-tracking of those with convictions for sex offences are launched and costed. Forms of identification using biometric techniques and visioning equipment to check for contraband are shown to have great possibilities in the criminal justice field. Closed circuit television cameras become the norm, so that in London it is estimated that each resident is filmed many hundreds of times each day.

So the really big market is not in prisons. In a world where the perception is that we live in constant danger, the big market is in security. Privately run prisons themselves may not be an exciting market but the potential for making money out of controlling risky people is huge. It is huge because the number of people who have no stake in society grows and such people are likely to be risky. Indeed the list of risk factors on the computerized system for risk assessment used by the English probation service includes a number of indicators of poverty, homelessness and disadvantage. So if you score highly on measures of poverty, you are by definition 'risky'. If you are risky you will be subject to more controls and thrust more deeply into the suspect part of the population.

Meanwhile traditional methods of social control through building social cohesion, setting up mutual associations and cooperatives, opening youth clubs, strengthening families, supporting parents, providing remedial education and offering job training are difficult to turn into a business and form into a basis for a market. So the pressure is on the hard-pressed municipal government to buy CCTV cameras to watch its young people rather than training a youth worker to engage with them. The company that sells the surveillance cameras has more power to lobby and to sell its wares than the small non-government organization that does neighbourhood mediation and brings families together in community activities. The company that sells lie-detector testing equipment for people convicted of sex offences has a lot more resources to advertise than the group of volunteers from the local church who offer to befriend and support such people in their local community on their release from prison.

Similarly the language of business infiltrates the crime control field just as it has infiltrated the prison field. Maybe it is not enough to privatize prisons and criminal record computer systems. What about crime control in the community, care homes for disturbed children, supervision of convicted people under probation orders? As governments accept these ideas, the organizations that make up the penal policy community disappear. If probation or social work is privatized, the organizations of probation and social workers disappear. As care of delinquent youth is privatized, the professional organizations for youth workers of various kinds no longer exist. The professionals may still be there, but now they are working for private companies. No longer can they work together in a professional association commenting on government policies, publishing magazines about their subject and how to improve it, speaking out about the ethical imperatives of their work. Thus the field of debate is narrowed. The government meets less opposition to the unworkable plans it may draw up. The public hears fewer voices setting out the realities of the impact of government policies as they affect the grassroots. The debate is impoverished.

The workers who joined the public sector with the intention of serving the community are silenced. Instead, commercial companies promote their products over those of their competitors. There will be no debate about principle. The argument will be solely about which company is most cost-effective. Those in government receive deputations of business people showing off their latest biometric devices. The ethics of the punishment business are stripped out: incarceration, control, surveillance, tracking, restricting people to one area or preventing them going to another become business items, to be tendered for, contracted for and delivered at the best price and with the hope of renewing the contract. The expansionary forces have a clear field in which to operate, with nothing in their way but their competitors. In 2004 it was announced in London that

> the 5,000 most prolific offenders in England and Wales are to be tagged and tracked using the global positioning system (GPS).... Operators at the control room, which would be run by the private company providing the device, would be able to track the person down to the nearest 100 yards, giving an accurate reading of the criminal's location. The scheme is likely to be similar to one already underway in Florida, US.... The scheme is run by Pro Tech, one of the leaders in satellite tracking technology.[105]

A Market in Criminal Justice – Some Implications

Between 1989 and 1998 spending on punishment by the State of Mississippi rose by 115 per cent. Spending on higher education by the state rose by less than 1 per cent. In the 1990s Mississippi built 16 new prisons. Six of them were privately run. It has built no new four-year colleges or universities for 50 years. Nearly 14,000 black men are in prison in Mississippi. Just over 7,000 are in four-year colleges and universities. It costs the State of Mississippi just under $7,000 a year to send someone to college. It costs over $10,000 a year to send someone to prison.[106] Mississippi is a poor state. More children live in poverty in Mississippi than in any other US state. More children are born to teenage mothers than in any other state. More teenagers die through murder, suicide or accidents.[107] Yet Mississippi has an imprisonment rate per 100,000 of its population of 682,[108] more than every nation state in the world apart from the United States itself. Two-thirds of the prisoners in Mississippi are in prison for non-violent crimes.[109] Nearly three out of four (72 per cent) of the state's prisoners are black.[110]

As governments adopt policies which use more of their money for punishment and crime control, there is less to spend on education, health, housing and poverty reduction. Societies become more unequal. The poor have less chance to climb out of their poverty and the next generation of prisoners is created, a larger group than the generation before. The crime control business is kept in business as the pool of risky people grows bigger.

Notes

1   From <www.moneycentral.msn.com>, 5 January 2005.
2   Martin Wolf, *Why Globalization Works*, New Haven: Yale University Press, 2004, p. xvii.
3   Joseph Stiglitz, *Globalization and Its Discontents*, Harmondsworth: Penguin, 2004, p. 221.
4   *Ibid.*, p. 248.
5   From <www.iol.co.za>, 27 January 2005.
6   Rick Telander, 'Your Sneakers or Your Life', <www.chuckconnection. com>.
7   Khatchik der Ghougassian, 'Changing Patterns of the Culture of Violence in Buenos Aires', in *Connecting Weapons with Violence: the South American Experience*, Monograph 25, Institute for Security Studies, South Africa, 1998.
8   Elliot Currie, 'International Developments in Crime and Social Policy: Market and Society and Social Disorder', in *Crime and Social Policy, Papers from an International Seminar held at Edinburgh University: 31 July – 2 August 1991,* London: NACRO, 1992, p. 107.
9   *Ibid.*, p. 114.
10 Roberto Briceño-Leon and Verónica Zubillaga, 'Violence and Globalization in Latin America', *Current Sociology* 50, 1 (January 2002), London, Thousand Oaks, CA and New Delhi: Sage Publications, p. 22.
11 Deepa Narayan *et al.*, *Voices of the Poor: Can Anyone Hear Us?,* Oxford and New York: Oxford University Press for the World Bank, 2000, p. 223.
12 *Ibid.*, p. 224.
13 Most Rev. Peter K. Screen, Archbishop of Kumasi, 'Poverty, the Bane of Freedom', Address to the International Commission of Catholic Prison Pastoral Care Congress, Ireland, 5–12 September 2003.
14 *The Justice Update,* 1, 2, Foundation for Human Rights Initiative, Uganda, 2004.
15 Deepa Narayan *et al.*, *Voices of the Poor*, pp. 25–6.
16 *Ibid.*, p. 273.

17   *Ibid.*, p. 222.

18   Elliot Currie, *International Developments in Crime and Social Policy*, p. 110.

19   Bob Deacon, *Globalization and Social Policy: the Threat to Equitable Welfare'* , Occasional Paper No. 5, United Nations Research Institute for Social Development, Geneva, March 2000, p. 2.

20   Elliot Currie, *International Developments in Crime and Social Policy*, p. 109.

21   International Labour Organization, *A Fair Globalisation, Creating Opportunities for All*, 2004, para 198.

22   Maarten Goos and Alan Manning, *Lousy and Lovely Jobs: the Rising Polarization of Work in Britain,* London School of Economics, 2003, p. 3.

23   Deepa Narayan *et al., Voices of the Poor*, p. 234.

24   *Ibid.*, p. 273.

25   Roberto Briceño-Leon and Verónica Zubillaga, *Violence and Globalization in Latin America*, p. 19.

26   The Gini index 'measures the extent to which the distribution of income (or consumption) among individuals or households within a country deviates from a perfectly equal distribution'. *Human Development Reports, Understanding the Data, Definitions of Statistical Terms*, United Nations Development Programme <www.hdr.undp.org>.

27   Pablo Fajnzy, Daniel Lederman and Norman Loayza, 'Inequality and Violent Crime', *Journal of Law and Economics,* 45, (April 2002), University of Chicago, p. 25.

28   Johan van Wilsem, 'Criminal Victimisation in Cross-National Perspective, an Analysis of Rates of Theft, Violence and Vandalism across 27 Countries', *European Journal of Criminology,* 1, 1 (January 2004), p. 106.

29   Joseph Stiglitz, *The Roaring Nineties: Seeds of Destruction*, London: Allen Lane, 2003, p. 295.

30   World Health Organization, *Small Arms and Global Health*, Geneva: WHO, 2001.

31   Michael Fleshman, 'Counting the Cost of Gun Violence', in *Africa Recovery*, 15, 4 (December 2001), p. 1.

32   *Ibid.*, p. 4.

33   *Ibid.*, p. 5.

34   Silvia Ramos and Julita Lemgruber, 'Urban Violence, Public Safety Policies and Responses from Civil Society', *Social Watch Report*, p. 136.

35   Deepa Narayan *et al., Voices of the Poor*, p. 222.

36   Roy Walmsley, 'Global Incarceration and Prison Trends', *Forum on*

Crime and Society, 3, 1–2 (December 2003), Vienna: United Nations Office on Drugs and Crime, p. 70.

37   Anne Fuller *et al.*, *Prolonged Pretrial Detention in Haiti*, New York: Vera Institute of Justice, 2002.

38   US Department of Justice, *Prisoners at Midyear 1995,* Washington DC: Bureau of Justice Statistics, 1996.

39   US Department of Justice, *Prison and Jail Inmates at Midyear 2004*, Washington DC: Bureau of Justice Statistics, 2005.

40   For a brief outline of the history of the involvement of private enterprise in imprisonment in the United States from 1607 onwards, see James Austin and Garry Coventry, *Emerging Issues on Private Prisons*, Washington DC: Bureau of Justice Assistance, pp. 9–11.

41   Christian Parenti, 'Privatized Problems: For-Profit Incarceration in Trouble', in Andrew Coyle, Allison Campbell and Rodney Neufeld (eds), *Capitalist Punishment: Prison Privatization and Human Rights*, Atlanta and London: Clarity Press and Zed Books, 2003, pp. 30–1.

42   President's Commission on Privatization, *Privatization: Toward More Effective Government*, Washington DC: US Government Printing Office, 1988.

43   US Department of Justice, US Department of Justice, *Prisoners in 2004*, Washington DC: Bureau of Justice Statistics, 2005.

44   US Department of Justice, *Prison and Jail Inmates at Midyear 2003*, Washington DC: Bureau of Justice Statistics, 2004.

45   US Department of Justice, US Department of Justice, *Prisoners in 2004*.

46   James Austin and Garry Coventry, *Emerging Issues*, p. ix.

47   'The GEO Group, Inc. Announces Opening of Hood Office in the United Kingdom', press release, 1 December 2004, <www.phx.corporate.ir.net>.

48   Jo Paterson, 'Private Justice for All', *Access: Security Issues for Business People* (Autumn 2003): 12, published by Securicor.

49   Julie Berg, 'Prison Privatization: Developments in South Africa' in Coyle *et al.* (eds), *Capitalist Punishment,* pp. 179.

50   Public Services International Research Unit, *Prison Privatisation Report International*, No. 69 (July 2005), London: University of Greenwich.

51   Lenny Roth, 'Privatisation of Prisons'.

52   Philip J. Wood, *The Rise of the Prison Industrial Complex in the United States* in Coyle *et al.* (eds), *Capitalist Punishment*, p. 16.

53   'Prison Ship Could Head for Thames', BBC News, 19 December 2004.

54   Wisconsin Department of Corrections, 'Inmate Disturbance at Whiteville Prison', press release, 30 November 1999.

55   Youssef Sawan and Kristian Knutsen, 'Counting Prisoners in

Wisconsin', *The Wisconsinite*, 22 June 2004.

56   Florence Correctional Facility, briefing report, <www.flpba.org/private/florence>.

57   John L. Clark, Corrections Trustee, *Report to the Attorney General – Inspection and Review of the Northeast Ohio Correctional Center,* 25 November 1998, p. 34.

58   Dartmoor prison in the West of England was built in 1809 for French captives during the Napoleonic wars and is still in use today.

59   For a detailed account of prison privatization worldwide, see Public Services International Research Unit, *Prison Privatisation Report International,* London: University of Greenwich. All issues of the Report are on <www.psiru.org/justice>.

60   Philip J. Wood, 'The Rise of the Prison Industrial Complex in the United States' in Coyle *et al.* (eds), *Capitalist Punishment*, p. 17.

61   Philip Mattera, Mafruza Kan and Stephen Nathan, *Corrections Corporation of America: a Critical Look at its First Twenty Years,* Grassroots Leadership, Corporate Research Project of Good Jobs First and Prison Privatisation Report International, 2002, p. 20.

62   *Ibid.*, p. 21.

63   *Ibid.*, p. 23.

64   Alex Friedmann, 'Juvenile Crime Pays – But at What Cost?', in Coyle *et al.* (eds), *Capitalist Punishment*, p. 49.

65   Philip Mattera, Mafruza Kan and Stephen Nathan, *Corrections Corporation of America,* p. 23.

66   John L. Clark, Corrections Trustee, *Report to the Attorney General.*

67   Philip Mattera, Mafruza Kan and Stephen Nathan, *Corrections Corporation of America,* p. 23.

68   John L. Clark, Corrections Trustee, *Report to the Attorney General.*

69   Cheryl W. Thompson, 'Must Stop Sending Inmates to Ohio Prison', *Washington Post*, 26 February 1998, quoted in Philip Mattera, Mafruza Kan and Stephen Nathan, *Corrections Corporation of America*, p. 24.

70   James Austin and Garry Coventry, *Emerging Issues*, p. 36.

71   John L. Clark, Corrections Trustee, *Report to the Attorney General.*

72   Dawn Moore, Kellie Leclerc Burton, and Kelly Hannah-Moffat, '"Get Tough" Efficiency: Human Rights, Correctional Restructuring and Prison Privatization in Ontario, Canada' in Coyle *et al.*, *Capitalist Punishment*, p. 159.

73   'T. Don Hutto Facility Receives Accreditation', *Taylor Daily Press*, 18 January 2005.

74   US Supreme Court, *Hutto v Finney 437 US 678,* 1978. See also Craig Becker and Amy Dru Stanley, 'The Downside of Private Prisons', *The Nation*, June 1985.

75   Public Services International Research Unit, *Prison Privatisation Report International July 1996*, London: University of Greenwich.

76   Department of Justice, 'Justice Department Sues, Files for Emergency Relief to Protect Juveniles in Louisiana's Jena Juvenile Justice Center', press release, Washington DC, 30 March 2000.

77   Elizabeth Alexander, 'Private Prisons and Health Care: the HMO from Hell' in Coyle *et al.* (eds), *Capitalist Punishment*, p. 72.

78   Her Majesty's Chief Inspector of Prisons, *Report on a Full Announced Inspection of HMP & YOI Ashfield 1–5 July 2002*, London: Home Office, 2002.

79   National Audit Office, *The Operational Performance of PFI Prisons*, Report by the Comptroller and Auditor General, HC Session 2002–2003: 18 June 2003, London: The Stationery Office, 2003, pp. 38–9.

80   *Ibid.*, p. 6.

81   Commission for Racial Equality, *A Formal Investigation by the CRE into HM Prison Service of England and Wales, PART 2: Racial Equality in Prisons*, London: CRE, 2003.

82   National Audit Office, *The Operational Performance of PFI Prisons*, p. 6.

83   Amanda George, 'Women Prisoners as Customers: Counting the Costs of the Privately Managed Metropolitan Women's Correctional Centre: Australia' in Coyle *et al.* (eds), *Capitalist Punishment*, p. 207.

84   Philip Mattera, Mafruza Kan and Stephen Nathan, *Corrections Corporation of America*, p. 24.

85   *Ibid.*

86   United States General Accounting Office (GAO), 'Private and Public Prisons: Studies Comparing Operational Costs and/or Quality of Service', Letter Report, 08/16/96, GAO/GGD-96-158, Washington DC.

87   *Ibid.*

88   James Austin and Garry Coventry, *Emerging Issues*, p. 38.

89   *Ibid.*, p. ix.

90   National Audit Office, *The Operational Performance of PFI Prisons*, p. 25.

91   *Ibid.*, p. 26.

92   *Ibid.*, p. 27.

93   *Ibid.*, p. 6.

94   *Ibid.*, p. 7.

95   *Ibid.*, p. 9.

96   Austin and Garry Coventry, *Emerging Issues*, p. ix.

97   Quoted in Philip Mattera, Mafruza Kan and Stephen Nathan, *Corrections Corporation of America*, p. 31.

98   *Ibid.*, p. 32.

99　'Position Paper on the Lesotho Prison Services', private communication.

100　'Case Study: Private Prisons', South African Institute of International Affairs, <www.saiia.org.za>.

101　Jo Paterson, 'Private Justice for All'.

102　Nils Christie, *A Suitable Amount of Crime*, London and New York: Routledge, 2004, p. 9.

103　See, for example, Ulrich Beck, *Risk Society: Towards a New Modernity*, London, Thousand Oaks, CA and New Delhi: Sage Publications.

104　'Electronic Tagging – an Alternative to Custody' in *Access: Security Issues for Business People* (Autumn 2003): 13, published by Securicor.

105　'A Prison without Bars', BBC News, 19 July 2004.

106　Grassroots Leadership, *Education v Incarceration: a Mississippi Case-study*, Charlotte, North Carolina, 2001, p. 1.

107　*Ibid.*, p. 2.

108　US Department of Justice, *Prison and Jail Inmates at Midyear 2004*.

109　Grassroots Leadership, *Education v Incarceration*, p. 3.

110　*Ibid.*, p. 4.

4

The 'War on Drugs' and Migration

An 82-year-old woman from Bogota who struggled economically to care for her mentally retarded son was convinced by narco-traffickers that one trip to New York as a 'drug mule' would supply her with enough money for her son's future.

But her dream ended when a pellet full of narcotics ruptured in her stomach as she got into a cab at John F. Kennedy Airport in New York. She died before the cab could reach a hospital.[1]

The policing of 'global flow' is criminalizing migrants and creating vast networks of illegal trafficking.

Saskia Sassen, 20 August 2003[2]

Crime, Drugs and Migration

In this chapter we look in close-up at two features of the modern world that have been brought within the crime sphere and affected it deeply, the drugs business and migration. Neither necessarily has anything to do with crime and criminals. Buying, selling and consuming substances that change mood or produce different states of consciousness has not always come into the criminal sphere. The First Opium Convention was in 1912. Even now the law is selective in choosing which mood-altering substances are illegal and which are not. Similarly, crossing borders without the right papers, moving from place to place and being subject to border controls has also not always been the subject of criminal sanctions.

It is not inevitable that these areas have been criminalized. Other approaches could have been applied and different policy choices made. The matter of certain drugs having undesirable effects on human health could have been dealt with in the way that cigarettes and alcohol are dealt with, that is by discouragement, regulation and high taxation, and many argue that regulation would be a more effective approach. Migration could be seen as a normal consequence of globalization rather than as a crisis. Its positive aspects for countries with ageing populations and its potential as an engine of economic growth could be decoupled from fears about crime and cultural identity, and it could be managed sensibly.

But in the world of today both are linked very closely with criminality, and the criminal justice systems of many countries are deeply affected by them. They merit a separate chapter because they differ so much from the control of those actions that have been regarded as crimes harmful to society since the time of Cain and Abel.

Terrorism, too, has led to the new definition of many acts as crimes. It has led to new repressive laws and to very harsh imprisonment conditions for some people. It needs fuller treatment than it is possible to offer here and will not be discussed.

The Drugs War

Let us begin with the illegality of certain drugs. As a global issue, drug control and its impact on people, on whole societies and on the environment merits more than one chapter in a small volume. So we shall concentrate on the effect of the 'war on drugs' on criminal law, criminal justice systems and the prison systems of the world. Crime and illegal drugs are connected at many points. Punishment and prisons are inextricably linked with the 'war against drugs'. If certain substances were not illegal and their possession and sale were not crimes, the prisons of the world would have empty places and courtrooms would close early. The prison populations of the world are boosted enormously by the imprisonment of those connected in some way with the drugs business. The running of prisons has been made more difficult and more dangerous by the imprisonment of many people connected with the drug business. Health risks have increased because of the use of infected needles to inject drugs. The massive system of control that stems from the United Nations drug conventions and imposes a harsh law enforcement regime on most countries has not prevented the drug market from flourishing, nor stopped many millions of people from buying and consuming illegal substances every minute of every hour of every day. According to figures from the United Nations, in 2001–3, 185 million people broke the drug laws of their countries. The percentage of the population of the world that has used an illicit drug at least once is 3 per cent, or 4.7 per cent of the world's population aged between 15 and 64. Cannabis was used by 146 million. Thirty million took amphetamines. Ecstasy was taken by over eight million and cocaine by thirteen million. More than fifteen million people took opiates, including heroin.[3] It is agreed that these UN figures are difficult to verify and are probably underestimates.

The Links between Illegal Drugs and Crime

The place to start this discussion is the link between illicit drugs and crime. Making it illegal to sell, possess or consume certain substances has created a huge number of new criminal acts. In some parts of the world it has been traditional for centuries for people to use certain substances that grow naturally in the environment.[4] The introduction of laws making use of these substances illegal has increased the number of people, often people from poor rural areas, coming into contact with the police and ending up in prison. In some countries very harsh punishments, including the death penalty, are used to respond to the use of these drugs. Anyone in any doubt about the link between illegal drugs and crime should take a look at the website of the Central Narcotics Bureau of Singapore. It sets out the position very clearly:

> Anyone caught in the possession of a certain amount of a controlled drug is presumed to be trafficking in the drug and the onus is on him to prove that the drug found on him is not for the purpose of trafficking...

There follows a table of punishments according to type of drug and nature of offence. Under the heading 'heroin' we read that for 'illegal traffic, import or export of heroin of more than 15 grams' the punishment is death. For 'possession and consumption', the punishment is 'up to S$20,000 fine or 10 years' imprisonment, or both'. Cannabis is also severely punished. For 'illegal traffic, import and export of cannabis of more than 500 grams' the punishment is death. For the 'illegal traffic, import and export of cannabis resin of more than 200 grams' the punishment is likewise death, as it is for the same offences involving a 'cannabis mixture of more than 1000 grams'. For 'possession and consumption of cannabis' the punishment is 'up to S$20,000 fine or 10 years' imprisonment, or both'.[5]

Shanmugam Murugesu is a Singaporean who served for eight years in the Singapore Armed Forces and represented the country in international water-sports. Then he had family problems and fell on hard times. He had to bring up twin boys unaided. Now these twin sons, aged fourteen, are fighting for their father's life. He is under sentence of death for having trafficked a kilo of cannabis. His past criminal history is one minor traffic offence.[6] The boys are handing out leaflets in a shopping centre calling for their father's death sentence to be commuted to imprisonment.

Although it is rare for a drug trafficker to face the death penalty, many people are imprisoned, sometimes for lengthy terms, for possessing or selling drugs. But the consequences of these substances being illegal resonate further than that. Much other crime not involving possession and consumption is also related to the illegality of drugs. People who have little money and have become dependent on a drug will need to buy it and will therefore need to get money somehow. Other crimes such as robbery and theft provide the money they need. Stealing and robbing to get enough money for drugs is a common cause of crime. The BBC reported in 2004 that China has 1.05 million registered drug addicts. Many of them are unemployed, migrant workers or farmers. According to Chinese sources 80 per cent of the men are involved in crime and 80 per cent of the women are working as prostitutes.[7] A survey in the United States published in 1997 reported that nearly one in five of prisoners in state prisons and 16 per cent in federal prisons admitted to committing their crimes to get money to buy drugs.[8]

The illegality of the drug business creates yet another layer of crime and violence. The drug business is an illegal business. Therefore, the normal rules that regulate businesses do not apply. Since this is an illegal market, the business can only be regulated by violence. Thus gun crime and gun deaths become more common in the poorer areas of towns and cities. In Latin America much of the violence and gun crime of the cities is tied to the drug trade. Two Latin American sociologists have argued that in the 1990s the drug trade became more sophisticated. The distributors paid the sellers not in money but in more drugs, which had to be sold to make a profit. Many individual sellers became involved and intense competition for the markets followed. The distributors also paid in guns, and high levels of violence were the outcome.[9]

The prison populations of the world are affected by all these factors. The laws making the drug business illegal have led to a great increase in the number of prisoners. The need to get money for drugs has increased the rates of crimes such as burglary and robbery, which lead to imprisonment. The violence and spread of gun ownership associated with the drug market have boosted the number of those convicted for crimes of violence.

The War on Drugs Fills the Prisons

It is not possible to make an accurate assessment of the total number of the prisoners of the world who are imprisoned because of the drug laws, but we can make some rough estimates. We know that, of the 2.25 million prisoners in the United States, at least 450,000, that is around 20 per cent, are in prison for a drug offence.[10] Punishments for drug offences in the US are harsher than in many other countries so the 20 per cent cannot be applied across the board, but even if a conservative estimate of 10 per cent is made, we are still talking about nearly one million people worldwide. In addition to that percentage we have to add the unknown number of prisoners whose route to prison was crime to get money to buy drugs, or violence associated with the drug market. It was estimated in 2003 that at least half of the 365,000 prisoners in the fifteen countries of the European Union had a history of using illegal drugs.[11] In February 2004, a report published by the Ministry of Justice of Portugal noted that, of those in prison, at least four in ten were locked up because of crimes connected to illegal drugs.[12]

In Canada in 2000 more than one in four of all federal prisoners (those serving two years or more) were in prison for a drugs offence.[13] In England 16 per cent of men and 40 per cent of women are imprisoned for a drugs offence.[14] One organization suggests that about a quarter of the world's prison population is imprisoned because of some connection with drugs illegality.[15] This estimate is not far-fetched if we add together those described as guilty of a drug offence and those deemed to have committed a crime because they needed to buy drugs, or had some other involvement in the business.

Nikhat is nearly 25.... She has been in prison for five months. She is from a small and poor family.... Nikhat was married when she was fifteen. Her husband has been in Lucknow jail since three years.... She and her husband both worked as labourers and earned just sufficient to make both ends meet. She said that they got into drug peddling because whatever she earned was not enough.[16]

Crimes connected with illegal drugs fill the prisons of the world, not with the major players in the business, but with the many smaller participants, such as Nikhat from India: people with few opportunities who are presented with an illegal option that would make an enormous difference to their lives. A particularly sad and vulnerable group are the people, most of them indigent women from poor countries, who are persuaded to carry something with the lure of enough money to put a child through school or to open a small trading business. The situation of these poor women, often called 'drug mules', illustrates well the illogicalities and injustices of the drug laws.

According to Orlando Tobin, a Colombian who has set up a charitable enterprise in New York to arrange burials for drug mules who die in the process, 'drug mules usually carry about two pounds of narcotics in 18 to 25 pellets. A pellet consists of a condom or latex glove stuffed with the drugs.' Apparently the pellets are difficult to swallow and the carriers take a substance that numbs and loosens their throats. When they arrive at their destination they are met by one of the organizers of the drug deal who takes them to a hotel where they stay until the drugs have left their bodies. They are usually given laxatives to help in the process. If one of the condoms or gloves bursts the carrier will probably die of a drug overdose.[17]

In the United Kingdom a similar issue arises with women from Jamaica. Barbara is a fairly typical example. She is a mother of six children. She comes from Jamaica and at present lives in a small prison in the English Midlands. She was a vendor on the streets of Kingston when she was approached and told there were ways of making much more money. She agreed and went to a house where she was told how to swallow one hundred little parcels of cocaine. She managed to swallow 52 of them. She was given $700 and told she would get more money (another $3,000) in England. By the time she was on the plane she had decided against the enterprise and started eating in the hope she could pass all the drugs through her system in the toilet. She failed and when she landed she told customs officers what she was carrying. Customs at European airports now have see-through toilets where customs officers can watch and retrieve the drugs as they are excreted. After this had been done, Barbara went to a local hospital for an x-ray and they found that one package remained. She was eventually sentenced to three years and nine months in prison, a shorter sentence than is usual. The people who gave her the drugs to carry were not happy that she had not turned up to meet them with the drugs. They assumed she had stolen them. They kidnapped her brother, stabbed him and burnt him alive.[18]

About one in ten of all women in English prisons is a Jamaican. Yet their contribution to the amount of cocaine entering the country is small. A *Guardian* newspaper correspondent writes:

Compared with the total flow of cocaine into Britain – 40 to 50 tonnes a year is a customs estimate – the amount smuggled in by individual couriers is a minor link in the supply chain. The government's cocaine strategy admits that the vast bulk – about 85 per cent – arriving in Britain every year comes in container ships direct from Colombia or is shipped to Spain and then arrives at Britain's east coast ports by way of the Netherlands. The remaining 15 per cent brought in by air couriers is significant but it is only a minor stream feeding the river.[19]

As with crime more generally, it is not punishment of the small fry that is likely to reduce the harm. Other measures are more likely to make an impact. The journalist continues:

[T]he decision by the British authorities to pay for scanning equipment at Kingston's international airport makes more sense in spotting the swallowers before they get on the plane.... A major urban economic regeneration drive in the ghettos of Kingston might actually be more effective in tackling Britain's supply of cocaine than incarcerating young Jamaican women in Britain.

It would seem that the whole business of poor people importing drugs and being imprisoned benefits no one. This is not entirely so.

With the help of the British authorities the Jamaican government is reported to be looking at buying a privately run prison to lock up the drug mules deported from the UK. The British High Commissioner in Jamaica said, 'A number of British companies are interested, and we hope that it will happen soon.'[20]

American 'Exceptionalism' Again

In 1986 one in ten of the prisoners in US state prisons was there for a drug offence. By 1995 the figure had grown to 23 per cent.[21] In the United States the laws on drugs are some of the harshest in the world. Many states have mandatory minimum sentences for crimes involving drugs. In 1991 an American woman called Julie Stewart founded a new organization, Families Against Mandatory Minimums. Julie Stewart had a brother who grew a marijuana plant in a garage in Washington State. For this, his first offence, he was sentenced to five years in federal prison without parole. The sentencing of her brother drove Julie Stewart to set up her organization, which campaigns against harsh drug laws in the United States.

One of the people whose case is the basis of a campaign is Steven Treleavan. Steven was sentenced to twenty years in prison in Idaho for growing marijuana plants to provide his brother, who had AIDS, with a pain-relieving drug. The ten years mandatory minimum was doubled to twenty years because Steven had prior convictions for drug possession. In 1993, a year after Steven was sentenced, his brother died. Another campaign seeks justice for Barbara Dykes. When she was a teenager Barbara got involved in her boyfriend's drug distribution activities. A court in Georgia sentenced her to nineteen years and seven months in prison.[22] In 2002 the Governor of New Mexico commuted the prison sentence of a woman who was sentenced to 25 years and six months in prison for forging a prescription to get codeine-based painkillers.[23]

In the United States the laws against illicit drugs are full of codicils and amendments that increase the punishments that have to be given by the judges. In New Jersey, for instance, there is a 'drug free school zone law'. Conviction for distributing or even possessing drugs near a school brings with it a three-year mandatory minimum sentence. Any institutions where young people gather, such as day care centres or training projects, have been defined as schools. Many people living in inner-city areas where buildings are concentrated therefore find themselves living in a drug-free school zone where the punishments are higher. Those living in the outer city's more spacious residential districts are less likely to be affected.[24] The people in the inner city are likely to be black, Latino and poor. The people in the suburbs are less likely to be so. In England and Wales a similar law went through Parliament in 2005[25] after a minimal amount of parliamentary discussion and in the face of strong opposition from the main organizations concerned with effective drug policies.

The punishment for being involved with drugs in the United States reaches beyond prison. Under a law of 1998, people with a drug conviction lose their eligibility for federal financial aid for education. Between 1998, when the act containing this provision came into law, and 2005 more than 160,000 students were refused financial help with their studies. Since African-Americans make up more than half of those convicted of drug crimes, this provision is another element in the discrimination that characterizes the system.[26]

Drug Policies Make Prisons Worse

In recent years the connections between prisons and illegal drugs have become a more pressing problem for all prison administrations. The prisons fill up with people using or addicted to drugs. The culture of many prisons is overshadowed by the culture of drug taking. Prison health services are overwhelmed by the health needs these prisoners present. In Scotland, all prisoners entering prison over a twelve-month period were tested to see if they had drugs in their system when they arrived. Three-quarters tested positive.[27]

The prison health service in England and Wales carries out 50,000 detoxifications a year of prisoners who arrive in prison under the influence of drugs.[28] In one English prison six women who used drugs killed themselves within one year.[29] Some prison systems provide substitutes such as methadone for their drug-dependent prisoners. Others do not.

Not all prisoners enter prison dependent on drugs. However, prison is a place where the temptation to take something that eases the pain of imprisonment is great and the opportunities to do so are available. Many come to prison not using drugs and leave doing so. In Russia, research tells us that 13 per cent of those prisoners who injected drugs began injecting whilst in prison.[30] It is estimated that the percentage of prisoners in Europe who first started to inject drugs whilst in prison ranges from 7 per cent to 24 per cent.[31] In Iran there are about 2 million drug users and around 200,000 of these inject. Many of them are in prison, and HIV infection is spreading through the use of shared needles. One ex-prisoner with HIV, now working in a prison as a volunteer to help others in the same situation, told the BBC that 'Sometimes as many as 500 people use the same syringe. No one knows or cares about the consequences.'[32]

The drug business opens up many opportunities for corruption in prison systems. One of the consequences of drug illegality is an increase in the danger and violence of prison life. It intensifies the subordination of the addicted prisoners to the prisoners who control the supplies. It increases the spread of disease through the sharing of needles. The battle to stop the illegal drugs coming in leads the authorities to take measures that greatly worsen the treatment of prisoners. To stop prisoners getting hold of drugs during family visits grilles are placed between the prisoner and the family members when they visit. Many prisons perform regular tests to check if prisoners are taking drugs. The tests may require prisoners to urinate in front of prison staff to ensure that samples are not falsified for the drug testing. In the women's prison in Mauritius, women sentenced for a drug offence are not able to touch or hug their children, sometimes for many years.[33]

The Role of the United Nations

The United Nations plays a greater role in the control of illicit drugs than in many other areas of global threat, such as climate change or environmental pollution. The UN has the objective of eradicating completely or substantially reducing illicit drug markets. To that end it operates a system of control based on three main UN conventions. These conventions allow the use of narcotic and psychotropic substances for medical and research purposes only. Otherwise, it is the duty of UN member states to ban the production, distribution and use of these substances. Most member countries of the United Nations have signed the conventions and imposed the bans.

The UN is optimistic about the success of its work in eradicating illicit drug use. It argues that the diffusion of drug use into the general population has been contained and notes that only 3 per cent of people in the world use drugs, compared with 30 per cent who use tobacco.[34] However, it admits – and the figures given in its report for 2004 confirm – that the goal of eradication has not yet been achieved. Overall, according to the figures given to the UN by 96 member states, 6 per cent of countries reported a large decrease in illicit drug use and 17 per cent some decrease in use. Of the rest, nearly a half (46 per cent) reported an increase and 31 per cent reported no change.[35]

The UN brooks little disagreement with either its view of the need to control drugs or its methods. Its 2004 report is scathing about the 'paradoxical actions of a small, yet very vocal, number of actors' who 'break ranks and challenge the spirit of multilateralism'.[36] Some countries accept the UN framework but emphasize treatment, prevention and harm reduction. Others concentrate on enforcement. The countries that put more emphasis on treatment, prevention and harm reduction are subject to regular criticism from the UN's International Narcotics Control Board. In its comments on Europe in the 2004 report, the Board was not pleased with much of what was going on. In Europe, it notes, 'the public debate over cannabis use is dominated more by its alleged potential benefits than by its risks'.[37] Some countries faced criticism for their policy of providing injecting facilities or rooms. The Board says: 'drug injection rooms are against the central principle embodied in the international drug control treaties, namely that the use of drugs should be limited to medical and scientific purposes only'.[38] The Board notes that the European Parliament approved a proposal on penalties for drug trafficking and urges implementation, stating that 'member States of the European Union must take the necessary measures to ensure that serious trafficking offences are punishable by effective, proportionate and dissuasive criminal penalties.'[39] The Board also expressed concern about the 'medical use of cannabis in Canada and the Netherlands and in some jurisdictions of the United States'.[40]

Perhaps the severest criticism made against Europe is lack of fervour. 'During the past few years,' says the report, 'the Board has noted an ambiguity towards drug abuse in some countries in Western Europe.' Allegedly, 'authorities have not taken measures against incitement to abuse drugs'. Countries are supposed to have laws making it a criminal offence to incite anyone to take illicit drugs. These laws are in place in most countries but the Board is not confident about how seriously they are taken. '[I]t remains to be seen how these provisions are being implemented,' it says.[41] It is very critical of an opinion issued by the Supreme Court in Spain saying that advertising cannabis seeds and equipment for the growth of cannabis plants was not illegal because it was not for the purposes of trafficking. The Board is not happy with the medical prescription of heroin. It 'reiterates its reservations'.[42] Its strongest censure is reserved for the Netherlands. Its famous 'coffee-shops' (where cannabis is freely available) are 'contrary to the provisions of the international drug control treaties'.[43]

The cost of the emphasis on enforcement encouraged by the United Nations is not cheap. It is estimated that the United States spends $30 billion a year on enforcing its drug laws. The UK spends over £1 billion (nearly US$2 billion). It is estimated that the world spent between US$2 billion and US$6 billion over three years trying to reduce the amount of coca grown in Colombia.[44] The money spent on drug law enforcement could treat the addicts of the world many times over. Research shows that expenditure on treatment achieves much better results than enforcement. The Rand Corporation, in a report prepared for the US Office on Drug Control Policy and the US Army, considered the most effective way to reduce the number of cocaine users by 1 per cent. Spending the money in a country that produces cocaine to reduce the product would cost $2.6 billion. Spending it on preventing trafficking would cost $964 million. Spending it on enforcement of the drug laws at home would cost $675 million. To get a reduction of 1 per cent by treating people addicted to cocaine would cost $155 million.[45]

Again we see the pattern that has been emerging throughout this book. Huge sums of money are spent on enforcement and repression. Enforcement catches the small fry but not the major players, who continue their activities with impunity. The money is found for enforcement but not for the services of prevention, treatment and solution of the problem by attending to its root causes.

The Criminalization of Migration

The same pattern can be found in the world's response to migration. Drugs are unwanted substances. Refugees and immigrants are becoming unwanted people. More and more, those who flee persecution or who move from dire poverty to seek a better life are being treated in the same way as those who have been convicted of breaking the criminal law. The response of the richer countries to refugees and migrants has been increased enforcement and repression. Wary of unscheduled immigrants, rich countries place officials in foreign airports to check those attempting to leave. The borders of the European Union have been strengthened with equipment that detects suspected immigrants when they are still miles away. The seas are full of powerful boats looking for illegal, leaky crafts crammed with desperate people. Since it is now so difficult to enter the rich world without resources, refugees and migrants turn to traffickers. A new and very lucrative business has been created.

In Chapter 3 we described the forces that have led to an increase in crime and violence in those countries where for millions 'globalization has not worked'. These same forces that lead to crime and violence have also led to many people fleeing from terror and persecution or from social disorder and dire poverty. They have led to what some commentators now call 'people flow'.[46]

In Europe, the United States and Australia detention centres have sprung up, often run by the same commercial companies that run private prisons, where the treatment of the people in them is very similar to, or worse than, the treatment of prisoners. Migreurop is a group of people from France, Italy and Belgium campaigning against the setting up throughout Europe of detention centres for people who, according to them, are 'non-European citizens who have committed no offence other than crossing or trying to cross a border without papers'.[47]

There is ample material for a campaign. Throughout Europe the stories are the same. In Italy a case was brought against the manager and seven members of staff of a *centro di permanenza temporanea* (centre for migrants awaiting expulsion) for ill-treating detainees in 2002. In 2004 seven migrants attempted to escape from such a centre. After the escape attempt several detainees were beaten by the staff of the centre. Two months later, there was a disturbance at a similar centre in Calabria.[48] The Anti-Racist Initiative in Berlin noted 55 attempts at self-harm or suicide in the deportation prison in Berlin-Köpenick in the first four months of 2003.[49] The Italian branch of the doctors' organization Médecins Sans Frontières was banned from visiting immigration detention centres in Italy after publishing a report in January 2004 listing inadequate buildings, limited contact with the health service, insufficient legal and psychological help, abuses in the use of psychiatric drugs and excessive interventions by law enforcement officers.[50] An inquiry by the Prisons and Probation Ombudsman into conditions and treatment at an immigration removal centre at Oakington in England in 2005 found racism, violence and abuse. He described the centre as having 'a subculture of nastiness'.[51]

Deportation and removal are particularly controversial. In Finland in the summer of 2002 a mother, an eleven-year-old girl and a twelve-year-old boy were forcibly injected with sedating medication before being deported to the Ukraine.[52] In December 2003 a court in Brussels found four former Belgian police officers guilty of assault, battery and negligence in the case of Semina Adamu. She was on a plane going to Lagos with her ankles shackled. When her face was pushed into a cushion and held there, she became unconscious and died later in hospital from suffocation. One of the officers told the court that force was necessary 'to avoid disturbing other passengers'.[53] In February 2004 three German police officers went on trial accused of involuntary manslaughter of a Sudanese asylum seeker. Amir Ageeb was suffocated to death on a Lufthansa plane after it had left Frankfurt.[54]

Peter Qasim was 31 in May 2005. He did not have much of a birthday party. His last seven birthdays have been spent in an immigration detention centre in Australia. He is from Kashmir. His father was a separatist activist who was murdered by Indian security forces when Peter Qasim was a small child. When he was seventeen Peter, too, was arrested and tortured. He went into hiding, managed to get to Pakistan and eventually got to Australia. In Australia all those who seek asylum are locked up, regardless of the strength of their case or their past experiences. He has been held in five different detention centres and he spent his thirty-first birthday in Baxter, a centre in the South Australian desert. He has been refused acceptance as a refugee but India will not take him back. He has nowhere to go, so he stays in detention.[55]

Many children have been held in Australian detention centres to the detriment of their health and development. One three-year-old, Naomi Leong, whose mother is from Malaysia, was born in detention and spent her whole life there. She showed symptoms of serious disturbance. A child psychiatrist tried to persuade the government that she should be allowed out to attend a playgroup for two hours a day but the request was refused.[56] A federal court judge found against the government in the case of two Iranians who had spent years in detention centres. The judge deemed that the government had failed in its duty of care by failing to transfer them to a psychiatric hospital. One of them had repeatedly cut himself with a razor.[57] Not all of those seeking asylum in Australia reach it. Those captured by the Australian navy at sea were for some years taken to Nauru, a barren island, or to Papua New Guinea. In return for substantial aid from the Australian government, these countries provided detention for asylum seekers.

Australia has gone further than other Western countries in turning refugees and asylum seekers into criminals. In 1992 it brought in a law requiring that anyone who arrived in Australia by boat was to be incarcerated until granted a visa or leaving the country. The law was passed in 1992 but it was made retrospective to November 1989.[58] As a consequence, whole families have been locked up for years in detention centres built in remote places, where access for visitors and lawyers is difficult and where the protections offered to those in the normal prison system do not apply. Hunger strikers are force-fed. Chemical restraints are used. Isolation is used frequently.[59] In 1997 the management of all the centres was handed over to private companies. In 2001 the punishment for escaping from a centre was increased and strip searches of detainees became permissible.[60] In 2002 the United Nations sent a distinguished Indian judge to study the situation. He concluded that they were prisoners without having committed any offence.[61]

In May 2003 a group of doctors, psychologists and psychiatrists started publishing information on the effects of immigration detention on the detainees. They studied a sample of families who had been detained on average for two years and four months. They found that one-third of the detainees had harmed themselves in some way. Every one of the adults was suffering from depression. All the children had at least one psychiatric illness. More than half of the children talked of suicide. Nearly a quarter of the children had slashed their wrists or banged their heads violently against a wall. One of the doctors said that the form of detention used in Australia would inevitably be psychiatrically damaging.

> The asylum seekers know they are innocent people, and no aspect of the current system has any care or compassion. On the contrary they feel that they are hated, and that the authorities will do everything in their power to return them back to where they fled from.[62]

In December 2003 four detainees on Nauru sewed their lips together in a hunger strike.[63] Up to 90 per cent of the people held outside Australia or in the detention centres have been found to be genuine refugees.[64]

Here again we see evidence of what Nils Christie has called the sponge effect: 'crime … is like a sponge. The term can absorb a lot of acts – and people – when external circumstances make that useful.'[65] Choices are being made by nation states – and, in the case of illicit drugs, through the UN – to make more human activities into crimes and to react with repression and punishment rather than prevention, problem solving and the reduction of harm. The choice of which acts to make into crimes is not made on the basis of the amount of harm to humanity. Corporate activities such as money laundering and huge frauds, or environmental activities that damage the world, are not the priority. It is the crimes of the poor and the marginalized that receive the most attention from the law makers of the world.

Notes

1 'Caring for "Drug Mules" Who Perish on the Job: Colombian Aids Forgotten Victims', MSNBC News, 25 May 2004.

2 Saskia Sassen, 'A Universal Harm: Making Criminals of Migrants,' <www.opendemocracy.net>, 20 August 2003.

3 United Nations Office on Drugs and Crime, *2004 World Drug Report*, Vienna, 2004, p. 8.

4 See Axel Klein, Marcus Day and Anthony Harriott (eds), *Caribbean Drugs: from Criminalization to Harm Reduction*, Kingston: Ian Randle and London and New York: Zed Books, 2004.

5 See <www.cnb.gov.sg>.

6 Reuters, 'Twins Campaign to Free Father from Death Row', Singapore, 12 April 2005.

7 BBC News, 13 February 2004.

8 Office of National Drug Control Policy, *Drug-Related Crime Factsheet*, Washington DC, 2000, p. 3.

9 Robert Briceño-Leon and Verónica Zubillaga, 'Violence and Globalization in Latin America', *Current Sociology*, 50, 1 (January 2002): 24, London, Thousand Oaks, CA and New Delhi: Sage Publications.

10 Vincent Schiraldi and Jason Zeidenberg, *Costs and Benefits? The Impact of Drug Imprisonment in New Jersey*, Washington DC: Justice Policy Institute, 2003, p. 4.

11 European Monitoring Centre for Drugs and Drug Addiction, *Drugs in Focus: Treating Drug Users in Prison – a Critical Area for Health Promotion and Crime Reduction Policy*, Lisbon, 2003.

12 Alison Roberts, 'Portuguese Prisons "worst in EU" ', BBC News, 16 February 2004.

13 Larry Motiuk and Ben Vuong, 'Profiling the Drug Offender Population in Canadian Federal Corrections', *Forum on Corrections Research*, 13, 3 (January 2001): 25.

14 Michael Spurr, 'Is Imprisonment Dealing with Addiction?', *Prison Service Journal*, 156 (2004): 5.

15 See Transform, *After the War on Drugs: Options for Control*, London, 2004, p. 11.

16 Rani D. Shankardass and Saraswati Haider, *Barred from Life, Scarred for Life: Experiences of Women in the Criminal Justice System*, Gurgaon: Penal Reform and Justice Association (PRAJA), 2004, p. 191.

17 'Caring for "Drug Mules"'.

18 Audrey Gillan, 'Bursting Point: the Drug Mules in UK Prisons', *Guardian*, 30 September 2003.

19 Alan Travis, 'Punishment Solution May Lie Closer to Home',

Guardian, 1 October 2003.

20 Audrey Gillan, 'Bursting Point'.

21 Craig Haney and Philip Zimbardo, 'The Past and Future of U.S. Prison Policy: Twenty-Five Years After the Stamford Prison Experiment', in *American Psychologist*', 53, 7 (July 1998) p. 715.

22 See www.famm.org.

23 Drug Policy Alliance, newsletter, 29 August 2002, <www.drugpolicy.org>.

24 Vincent Schiraldi and Jason Zeidenberg, *Costs and Benefits?*, p. 14.

25 Drugs Act, 2005, Chapter 17.

26 Students for Sensible Drug Policy, 'Repeal the Higher Education Act Drug Provision', 2005, <www.ssdp.org>.

27 Scottish Executive, *Scottish Prison Service Annual Report and Accounts 1999–2000, Appendix 12*, Edinburgh, 2000.

28 International Centre for Prison Studies, *Prison Health and Public Health, the Integration of Prison Health Services,* conference report, London, 2004, p. 9.

29 'How Detox and Self-help Brought Suicide Jail Back from the Brink', *Observer*, 25 April 2004.

30 Lizz Frost, Vladimir Tchertkov and Murdo Bijl, 'Prisoner Risk-taking in the Russian Federation', report in *Prison Healthcare News*, 1 (Spring 2002), International Centre for Prison Studies, London.

31 Heino Stöver, *Drugs and HIV/AIDS Services in European Prisons,* Oldenburg: Bibliotheks und Informationssystem der Carl von Ossietzky Universität, 2002, p. 33.

32 'Iran's Drug Users Face AIDS Risk', BBC News, 28 November 2003.

33 International Centre for Prison Studies, 'Mission Report' (unpublished), 2001.

34 United Nations, *World Drug Report, 2004*, p. 7.

35 *Ibid.*, p. 9.

36 *Ibid.*, p. 7.

37 United Nations, *Report of the International Narcotics Control Board for 2004*, Vienna, p. 72.

38 *Ibid.*, p. 77.

39 *Ibid.*, p. 73.

40 *Ibid.*, p. 28.

41 *Ibid.*, p. 31.

42 *Ibid.*, p. 33.

43 *Ibid.*, p. 36.

44 Marcus Roberts, Axel Klein and Mike Trace, *Towards a Review of Global Policies on Illegal Drugs,* Drugscope for the Beckley Foundation, 2004, p. 2.

45 C. P. Rydell and S. S. Everingham, *Controlling Cocaine*, Rand Cor-

poration, 1994, p. 36.

46 See the debate 'People-Flow: Migration in Europe', on the website <www.opendemocracy.net>.

47 Migreurop, 'From European Migration and Asylum Policies to Camps for Foreigners', <www.migreurope.org>.

48 'Seven Migrants Escape from the Detention Centre in Bologna', Statewatch News Online, <www.statewatch.org>.

49 'Germany's Refugee Politics and Its Deadly Consequences: 1993 to 2003', Statewatch News Online, <www.statewatch.org>.

50 'Medici Senza Frontiere (MSF) Publishes a Damning Report on Conditions in Italy's Detention Centres for Foreigners', Statewatch News Online, <www.statewatch.org>, 26 January 2004.

51 *Inquiry into Allegations of Racism and Mistreatment of Detainees at Oakington Immigration Reception Centre and While under Escort*, report by the Prisons and Probation Ombudsman for England and Wales, London, July 2005.

52 Council of Europe, *Report to the Finnish Government on the Visit to Finland Carried Out by the European Committee for the Prevention of Torture and Inhuman or Degrading Treatment or Punishment (CPT) from 7 to 17 September 2003*, Strasbourg, 2004.

53 'Belgium: Four Belgian Police Officers Guilty over the Death of Semira Adamu', <www.statewatch.org>, 2003.

54 Deutsche Presse Agentur, 'German Police Tried for Sudanese's Death', 2 February 2004.

55 Kathy Marks, 'Australia Refuses to Relent over Detention of Indian Asylum Seeker', *Independent*, 13 May 2005.

56 Kathy Marks, 'Girl in Australian Detention Since Birth Suffers Mental Problems', *New Zealand Herald*, 6 May 2005.

57 Natasha Wallace and Joseph Kerr, 'Court Slams the Treatment of Detainees', *Sydney Morning Herald*, 6 May 2005.

58 Sharon Pickering, *Refugees and State Crime*, Leichardt, New South Wales: Federation Press, 2005.

59 *Ibid.*, p. 2.

60 *Ibid.*, p. 94.

61 *Ibid.*, p. 96.

62 Caroline Moorehead, *Human Cargo*, London: Chatto and Windus, 2005, p. 120.

63 *Ibid.*, p. 123.

64 *Ibid.*, p.125.

65 Nils Christie, *A Suitable Amount of Crime*, London: Routledge, 2002, · pp. ix–x.

5

'In the Name of Justice':
Is There a Better Way?

A criminal offence has caused a breach in relationship and the purpose of the penal process is to heal the breach, to restore good relationships and to redress the balance. Thus it is that we set out to work for reconciliation between the victim and the perpetrator. There may be sanctions such as fines or short exile but the fundamental purpose of the entire exercise is to heal. In the retributive justice process the victim is forgotten in what can be a very cold and impersonal way of doing things. In restorative justice both the victim and the offender play central roles. Restorative justice is singularly hopeful....

Archbishop Desmond Tutu, London, 2004[1]

Penal Reform in Retreat?

So far in this book we have looked at problems and failures, abuse and ill treatment, discrimination and injustice. We saw in Chapter 1 that imprisonment in most places is inhumane and damaging. It is intended to be a protection against crime and a way of reforming the deviant. Instead it becomes a machine for turning out more damaged and brutalized people. Chapter 2 showed us that whilst crime impacts most heavily on the poor, the criminal justice system fails to deliver protection or justice to most of those who seek its protection. Chapter 3 looked at the effects of commercialization, the introduction of buying and selling into crime control and what that means for defining crime and controlling criminals. Its effects have already been seriously damaging. Chapter 4 set out briefly the injustices that come from the 'war on drugs' and the strict control of migration.

We have to admit therefore that it is a bleak time for those who have spent their lives working inside the criminal justice system to improve it. Those working from outside for an end to its cruelties and the adoption of more socially beneficial policies may also feel very disheartened. The picture is grim. The use of imprisonment is growing. The known prison population of the world has grown by 12 per cent in the past six years. Most states assume their prison population will continue to grow and plan on that assumption. Punishments are becoming harsher, and the age group receiving the punishments has stretched to start younger and continue well into old age and even death. As we saw in Chapter 1, almost 32,000 prisoners in prisons in the United States are serving life without parole and can expect to die within the prison walls.[2] Crime is being used by politicians to stoke up fear and hatred. Social measures to contain crime are in retreat before an explosion of methods that control people but do not change them or improve their circumstances. Victims of crime are being used as political pawns but are not given the help and redress that would support them in dealing with what has happened to them. Children in trouble are being demonized and given harsh punishments rather than care and education.

These trends are evident in many countries and there is pressure on many politicians to move in these directions. If they do not make statements showing how tough they are, their opponents describe them as 'soft'. Countries that have had low prison populations such as Denmark are under pressure and their prison figures are rising. In France public opinion is traditionally sceptical about the effectiveness of prison but even there, harsh measures are being introduced for juveniles who break the law.[3] In Brazil a president dedicated to social justice was elected in 2002 yet prison reform is not on his agenda and the prison population in Brazil has risen hugely. The United Nations High Commissioner for Human Rights struggles to remind states of their human rights obligations but her voice is drowned out by the rhetoric about terrorism. Where prison reform was once a major item of discussion in ministries of justice, the talk now is of that new solution to prison problems, privatization. When prison reform was spoken of it was taken to refer to matters such as improving conditions, introducing staff training, and protecting prisoners' rights. Now when reform is discussed it means more efficiency, fewer staff, bigger prisons to get economies of scale and the use of the private sector.

In 1996 William Omaria, who was at that time the Minister of the Interior of Uganda, spoke at a conference in Kampala on penal reform. He was talking about what goes on in the prisons of the world and he said

> One day in the distant future people will probably look back on what happens in most countries today and wonder how we could do that to our fellow human beings in the name of justice.[4]

If we are to resist the trends described in this book and move towards a fairer system of criminal justice, we need to have a clear idea of how reform can be done, who should do it, and where helpful models can be found. In this chapter we shall be looking at what steps are being taken to change what is done 'to our fellow human beings in the name of justice', and what efforts are being made to link criminal justice to social justice.

Movements for Change

It is important to learn from success. We have seen the deep injustice of the death penalty, how it is used disproportionately against the poor and marginalized. The movement to abolish the death penalty is succeeding. New organizations to oppose it are active. Hands Off Cain, for example, is an organization of individuals and parliamentarians set up in 1993 at the European Parliament in Brussels. The aim of Hands Off Cain is to convince the UN to declare a moratorium on executions. Ensemble Contre la Peine de Morte (Together Against the Death Penalty) was established in France in 2000 and aims to establish a global policy against the death penalty. All the 46 member states of the Council of Europe have either abolished or declared a moratorium on the death penalty. Europe from the Arctic Circle to the Rock of Gibraltar and from the Republic of Ireland to Vladivostok is a death-penalty-free zone. Every year on average another three countries stop using the death penalty. In the US in 2003 the number of people on death row went down for the third year running.[5] Death penalty campaigners in the United States have gained some small victories, such as the decision by Governor Ryan of Illinois to commute all death sentences. In defending the decision, he said, 'Because the Illinois death penalty system is arbitrary and capricious – and therefore immoral – I no longer shall tinker with the machinery of death.'[6]

In March 2005 the US Supreme Court ruled the death penalty unconstitutional for those who committed their crimes when under the age of eighteen. This may seem a small step forward but it meant that 72 people were immediately removed from death row in the United States, though it must be added that life without parole for these young people was not deemed to be unconstitutional.[7]

The maintenance and promotion of human right standards in prisons is a movement with many supporters, and many countries are working to improve their treatment of prisoners. More than ever before, prisons are open to public scrutiny and public involvement. South Africa was a country where until a decade ago the prisons were harsh and militaristic. Nelson Mandela writes in his autobiography of the bleakness of his time in prison, the rare family visits in a bare room talking through glass under the flapping ears of five prison officers.[8] It is a symbol of the path taken by reform in prisons that now the University of KwaZulu–Natal is bringing its drama students into South Africa's prisons, not just into low-security and women's prisons but into the maximum-security section, to perform and discuss the meaning of what has been performed. The report of the project comments:

> They are prisoners – by definition they are excluded from society....
> [N]ow they are socialising, playing host to the students and engaging in candid conversations. It is especially emotional for the inmates to engage in discussion across class and ethnic groups. In addition, they are performing; and all performance is a risk. But it is positive risk-taking.[9]

When countries move from a totalitarian regime to democracy often one of the first changes that is made is ending secrecy about the prison system and giving members of the public and civil society organizations access to prisons. Prisons move from being closed state secrets to institutions in the public domain. They are no longer part of the military-repressive apparatus but become public institutions that provide information about themselves and welcome outsiders. Many countries have made that move and opened their prisons up to the outside world. Religious bodies, artists, social welfare, sports and counselling organizations, educators and befrienders are admitted. Journalists are allowed to visit to write about prisons and news and features about prisons start appearing in the media. Often prisoners are permitted to write to the newspapers for the first time.

Civil society involvement is a key element of the prison reform process. Without support from bodies outside the prison system, prison reform is unlikely to be sustainable. Prisons cannot be rehabilitative civilian institutions without the cooperation and support of the wider society. Prison systems that are open and accessible to a wide range of groups are more likely to uphold human rights standards. Prisons are less likely to be able to conceal human rights abuses if visitors are coming and going, talking to prisoners and visiting them where they are in the cells and workshops.

But reforming prisons is not enough. The concept of imprisonment and the punishment prisons inflict must be questioned. Across the world organizations and groups are working to find ways out of the retributive paradigm. Many are thinking about how punishment systems could continue to evolve and change. We have seen how in the past bodily punishments such as hanging, drawing and quartering were replaced by execution in private. In its turn execution became the exception and imprisonment took over as the main punishment. What is the next stage? What other methods of making people accountable for criminal acts could be developed? What method of punishment would be more appropriate for the twenty-first century? These questions are being asked.

In this chapter we look at developments that show a way out and counter current trends towards more crimes, more criminals, more punishment and less protection for the poor and marginalized.

Human Rights in Prisons

The pictures that circulated in 2004 from Abu Ghraib prison in Baghdad of Iraqi prisoners being ill-treated, humiliated, degraded and abused shocked the world. No justification was attempted. Treating prisoners in this way was not defended and is not defensible. The responsible authorities did not try to defend it. Instead they looked for someone to blame and for a source of blame as far from themselves as possible.

Most states in the world accept that prisoners should be treated according to the body of international human right laws and guidelines which derive from the International Covenant on Civil and Political Rights. More than one hundred states have ratified this treaty.[10] When they signed they agreed to treat prisoners with 'humanity and with respect for the inherent dignity of the human person'.[11] They agreed that trials should be fair.[12] They agreed to protect the right to life.[13] They agreed that torture and inhuman and degrading treatment must always be prohibited.[14] They agreed that all people who are arrested and charged should be seen as innocent until they are proved guilty.[15] They agreed to run their prisons according to a rehabilitative ideal.[16] As members of the United Nations they also agreed to take note of the guidance included in a range of more detailed instruments on how to treat prisoners and administer justice.[17] Many states have also agreed to the human rights requirements of their regional conventions and charters such as the American Convention on Human Rights and the African Charter on Human and Peoples' Rights.

We have seen how big the gap is between the standards set up by the world community and the reality. Chapter 1 gave examples from every region of the world of a failure to live up to those standards. But in spite of the high profile given to discussions about terrorism and the readiness of governments to chip away at the human rights protections, the movement to promote the treatment of prisoners with humanity and respect is not a movement in retreat. On the contrary, every year some substantial advance is made. There is a huge prison reform movement, involving people inside and outside the system, individuals and groups, professionals, religious and other campaigning groups, and ex-prisoners too. In every country there are people who do not accept that prisons should be places of dehumanization, disease and cruelty.

Reform from Inside

In Chile a wholesale reform of the prison system is being attempted, based on incorporating human rights principles. It was certainly needed. Before the changes, prison staff rarely entered the parts of the prison where prisoners lived. It was too dangerous. In May 2001 prisoners in a prison in northern Chile started a fire as a protest. The fire killed 26 prisoners. An inquiry found that two guards at the prison were too drunk to take appropriate action.[18]

Now much has been changed. When prisoners arrive in prison they get an information leaflet, a chance to telephone their families, and a proper medical examination. Clean sheets are issued. Cleaning materials are provided so that the cells are not so filthy. Health care has improved. The isolation cells are still used but they are less intimidating. More opportunities are provided for prisoners to work and the pay is better. Training is offered. Vulnerable prisoners who are at risk from the others get a chance to work and earn money. Local libraries have become involved with the prisons so that prisoners get books and there is more education. Social work students are getting involved in helping prisoners, and children are allowed to visit their imprisoned fathers. Better complaints procedures and information to prisoners about them and about their legal rights have been introduced. A special unit for pregnant women and mothers with babies has been set up and the juvenile prisoners have been separated from the adults. It is still possible that Chilean prisoners will be ill-treated; many will continue to feel unsafe and at the mercy of stronger prisoners; not all illnesses will be treated promptly and adequately. However, the changes listed above are measurable, and they contribute to a prison system that is more compliant to human rights.[19]

A former Vice-President of Costa Rica, Elizabeth Odio Benito, said in 2004:

> In all places where persons are deprived of their liberty, for whatever reason, there exists the potential risk of being subjected to torture, cruel, inhuman or degrading treatment or punishment.[20]

In order to prevent such ill-treatment there have to be bodies to ensure prisoners can complain and have their complaints heard. In South Korea a big change in the rights of prisoners took place in 2001. The government formally established a National Human Rights Commission. The terms of reference of the Commission allow it to enter any place of detention in order to investigate cases brought to its attention. Where it considers that a case is urgent it has the right to demand action to provide immediate relief pending its formal decision. In its first year of operation the Commission dealt with 1,113 complaints about the prison service. The major grounds of complaint raised included abuse of punishment, cruel treatment, improper medical treatment, restriction on sending letters or writing, and the use of abusive language by prison guards.[21]

Bringing in people from outside who have not worked in prisons is sometimes what is needed for reform. A fresh eye, an application of the values of the outside world to an unacceptable situation and an impatience with the deep-seated inertia that permeates prison systems can have a dramatic effect. In 1989 a professor of sociology took over as director-general of prisons in Poland and created a humane and progressive system. In Venezuela in October 2004 an army general took over as the new director-general of the troubled Venezuelan prison system. He immediately made a number of robust statements about the need to 'humanize' the system.[22] In November the Ministry of Justice announced a number of his decisions. He had got hold of 140 vehicles to improve the transfer of prisoners to court and to hospital so that prisoners could be brought to trial more quickly and sick prisoners could be treated properly. The Interior and Justice ministries are also pursuing improvements in the judicial system in order to speed up the time taken to bring a case to court. The Minister pointed out that the current problems largely affect the poor – those with money are able to gain faster access to justice and to release from prison. The amount of money for prison food doubled. Anti-violence measures were introduced and knives and guns were found and destroyed. NGOs will be brought into discussions about improving contacts between prisoners and their families and work is under way to move prisoners to prisons nearer their homes to help their social reintegration after release.[23]

We have seen how harsh the imprisonment of women can be. Imaginative ideas can be implemented. The governor of a women's prison in Scotland decided that children up to the age of five should be kept in prison with their mothers as part of a new experiment.

Up till then children were taken from their imprisoned mothers as soon as they were eighteen months old and given into the care of other members of the family or the welfare authorities. In the new system prisoners were to live with their children in independent houses on the edge of the prison grounds. The houses had a television, kitchen and garden but the mother would have to obey a curfew, report to the prison gate regularly and undergo drug testing. The prison governor said: 'I would like the mums to be able to do the same things I can with my children – to play with them and do their homework with them.'[24] In Australia, the governor of a prison for women rejected the rules of the prison because they were designed solely with men in mind. She produced a new set of rules that were more relevant to women.

Kazakhstan is a country that used to be full of prisoners. It probably had more prisoners per square kilometre than anywhere else in the world. The Russian prison system was often called the gulag, because the initials GULAG represent in Russian the initials of Main Camp Administration (the department that ran the prison camp system).[25] Kazakhstan was a place of exile within the Soviet Union and a major part of the gulag, with prison camps dotted all over its vast area. Kazakhstan became independent in 1991. Since then it has been going through a painful process of moving from a gulag system to a prison system more in accordance with humane values. The capital of this Central Asian republic is a new city called Astana. On the edge of Astana is a huge stone monument covered with the names of the prison camps where so many people met their deaths. The monument is dedicated to gulag victims.

In February 2004 Kazakhstan television showed footage of prisoners being severely beaten by prison staff at Arkalyk prison. The footage was allegedly recorded by one of the prison guards using a hidden camera. It showed several prisoners being made to stand spreadeagled against walls in the prison, and then being beaten with fists and truncheons, and kicked in the back and in the legs. The timestamp on the film indicated that it had been shot on two occasions in early and mid-January. Given the history of prisons in Kazakhstan, a cover-up and government denials might have been expected. But no. To its credit, the government set up an investigation and suspended the local officials pending its completion. The City Prosecutor started criminal proceedings against those allegedly responsible. On 25 February 2004 the director-general of Kazakhstan prisons and two other high-ranking officials resigned.[26] For Kazakhstan this was an indication of how far it had moved towards a prison system that was accountable and upheld standards governing the treatment of prisoners.

The right to life is a basic human right. Yet prisons are unhealthy places where diseases spread. Sometimes a prison sentence can be a death sentence. Many prisoners come from the groups in society with a high number of the untreated diseases of poverty and mental conditions that can lead to suicide. Veronique Vasseur is a French doctor who accepted an assignment as medical officer to one of the oldest prisons in Europe, La Santé in Paris. The assignment so shocked her that she wrote a book about it, published in 2000. She tells the story of how she was called to see a prisoner who was complaining that he could not eat. When she had him x-rayed, the pictures showed that he had swallowed a soupspoon, a fork, a bunch of five keys, 12 coins and a packet of razor blades.[27] Dozens of prisoners had a skin disease called bread scabies, which they got from eating mouldy bread.[28] A mentally ill prisoner went berserk in the segregation block. Dr Vasseur was called to assist. Only seven guards were there. They would not go in until there were eight. The eighth came. They opened the door and hurled themselves on top of the prisoner. The doctor found a bit of the prisoner's flesh in which to put the needle to give him an injection.[29]

The French Ministry of Justice had been aware for some time that their prison health care provision was grossly inadequate and it has now undergone a complete reform. Medical services in the prisons have been put under the control of the Ministry of Health rather than the Ministry of Justice and the local hospital now provides the primary health care for the prison. The amount of money spent has increased substantially and reports say that health care has improved.[30] A similar change took place in England and Wales in 2002.

In 2002 the high risk nature of the prison environment became very clear to 87 prisoners who were diagnosed HIV positive in Alytus prison, Lithuania. They were probably all people who injected drugs. When prison health officials carried out HIV tests on all the prisoners, they discovered that one-third were infected. It is suggested that all these prisoners shared needles to inject drugs. Before this discovery Lithuania had one of the lowest HIV infection rates in Europe.[31] The director-general of prisons lost his job and changes were introduced.

But the authorities in Lithuania still resisted the idea that they should accept they were holding people who would go to great lengths to inject drugs, and that drugs can always find their way into prisons. One way to combat this is to give prisoners access to clean needles. Lithuania is by no means the only country to find this solution too difficult. It is a solution that comes up against so many of the problems and prejudices of imprisonment. Prison authorities are not prepared to admit that their efforts to prevent drugs coming into the prison are not working. They cannot face the suggestion that it may be the prison staff themselves who bring in the illicit drugs. They fear that the needles may be used as weapons against them or against other prisoners. They fear above all to be seen to be condoning illicit drug use. Yet these attitudes condemn some prisoners to contracting a deadly disease in prison.

Some public health doctors and prison officials have braved this barrage of hostility and introduced schemes to give prisoners clean needles in exchange for used ones. In Spain, for instance, needle exchange programmes have been introduced into all prisons, for good reasons. Four out of ten Spanish prisoners are infected with hepatitis C and 15 per cent with HIV. In recent years in Spain many prevention measures were introduced: health information

campaigns, training, hepatitis B vaccination, methadone maintenance programmes and needle exchange programmes.

These measures have shown good results. Hepatitis B cases have
been greatly reduced. HIV infection was reduced from 32 per cent
in 1989 to 15 per cent in 2002 and hepatitis C from 46 per cent to
40 per cent between 1998 and 2001. After a successful pilot study,
needle exchange programmes were made available in all prisons.
The scheme allows any prisoner to ask for a clean needle. Once an
injecting kit has been given to a prisoner the rule is that it must be
returned before a new one is issued. Confidentiality must be
respected and prisoners must be informed that their participation in
the programme is confidential. Prison staff need to be reassured that
the programme increases their safety, since illicit hidden needles are
more dangerous to personnel than official needles in a plastic case.
In the case of an accident it is less likely that the syringe will have
been used and, if it has been used, it will be less likely that it has been
shared. Also, the more the prevalence of the disease can be reduced,
the safer the prison environment will be.[32]

Fighting for Reform from Outside

Those fighting for change within the system must overcome opposition from both politicians and their professional colleagues. For
those fighting from outside it is even more difficult. What is
happening in Japan is a good example of the sheer determination of
concerned citizens to improve their prisons. Although the rate of
imprisonment in Japan is low in international terms and prisoners in
Japan have enough to eat, well-lit cells and beds (or mats) to lie on
at night, the way they are treated has a harshness at its root that is not
often found elsewhere. Japanese prisoners may only talk at specified
times of the day. Few prisons have heating and some prisoners have
suffered frostbite during the winter. A standard punishment is the
use of a restraining device consisting of a belt with handcuffs at the
waist. Its result is that the prisoner cannot use his hands and has to

eat by lying on the floor and lapping at the food. Special trousers with a slit are provided to prisoners in the restraining belt and they have to carry out their toilet arrangements as best they can. Prisoners see their family visitors in small visiting booths divided by a perspex screen. On the prisoner's side are two seats, one for the prisoner and one for a prison guard. Solitary confinement is used to deal with prisoners deemed to threaten good order. Prisoners in solitary confinement are allowed two hours' exercise a week and may see only family members and lawyers.[33] An initial period of six months of such confinement can be extended by a further three months as often as prison authorities wish. Figures extracted from the Japanese government in 2002 showed that 26 prisoners had been living in solitary confinement for ten years or more. Four of them had lived that way for over 30 years and one for 38 years.[34]

Throughout the 1990s a small group of valiant campaigners worked hard for change. They published reports that were translated into other languages. They alerted international human rights bodies to what was happening. They presented reports to the United Nations.[35] None of this had any real effect.

Then in 2002 a scandal broke. It came to light that a prisoner had died in December 2001 after prison staff applied a high-pressure water hose to his rectum.[36] In May 2002 another prisoner died at the hands of prison staff. In this case the prisoner was placed in the restraining device with handcuffs and the belt was tightened to the point where his liver was damaged. A third prisoner suffered serious injuries in a similar way from the tightening of the belt. Five prison guards have been charged with offences relating to the deaths and the cases are going through the courts.[37] Following the scandal, the Minister of Justice apologized to the Japanese people for what had happened[38] and set up a reform committee to look into the system and make recommendations for change.[39] The Ministry also replaced the leather restraining belt with handcuffs lined with felt.[40] The Committee reported in December 2002. It made many recommendations.[41] One of these was that each prison should have a watchdog body similar to the Independent Monitoring Boards in England and Wales. This recommendation was accepted.

The problems of prisons in Kenya have been highlighted elsewhere in this book. In 2002 a joint delegation of officials from the Malawi and Kenya prison services visited Rajasthan in India. They were taken there by the NGO Penal Reform International to see the Indian system of open prisons, which has been in operation for over 40 years.[42]

Jagdish Prasad Sharma was a resident of such a prison. His day was not like the day of most prisoners. After breakfast he cleaned his truck and then drove it off to work at a stone quarry. When he got back again at seven in the evening his wife was at home waiting for him. Although he was living a normal life, in fact Jagdish Prasad Sharma was serving the last part of a fourteen-year sentence for murder.

The open jail where he lived is in Sanganer, about 25 kilometres from Jaipur, the capital of Rajasthan. It holds about 150 prisoners, including ten women. In Sanganer prison the prisoners have to build their own houses. They can go to work as long as the work is not further than ten kilometres from the prison, but must be back by seven in the evening. The children who live with them attend nearby schools.[43] By showing the system to people from Kenya and Malawi, Penal Reform International hoped that the idea of open prisons would spread to East Africa.

In France, large numbers of young people get involved in prisons through an organization called GÉNÉPI. This is an organization of students who go into prisons to teach prisoners seeking education either at the basic level or through the study of university subjects such as law, philosophy and economics. The students also get involved in creative activities such as theatre and music. Outside prisons GÉNÉPI volunteers work to counteract prejudice against ex-prisoners by involving schools and colleges in debates and organizing exhibitions, concerts and readings of literary works by prisoners. A regular GÉNÉPI newsletter aims to educate the public.[44]

Ex-prisoners' Organizations

Some penal reform organizations are founded by or consist mainly of ex-prisoners. Their work often concentrates on finding former prisoners somewhere to live, providing them with education and training and giving them support when they leave prison. Others take a higher-profile approach and aim to represent former prisoners in public debates and through comments to the media when a prison-related topic is in the news. Two former political prisoners in Iran were involved in setting up an organization, the Society for the Defence of the Rights of Prisoners (SDRP), which worked to protect detainees and promote prison reform. It established a small fund to provide free legal advice to prisoners and also supported the families of detainees.[45]

In Australia a group founded by ex-prisoners called Justice Action campaigned in the 2004 Australian general election for the voice of prisoners to be heard. Untried prisoners and those serving a sentence of three years or less are eligible to vote. Justice Action worked to ensure that the eligible prisoners were registered.[46]

The Contribution of Individuals

Father José Luis Tellez is a priest in a poor part of Mexico City. He runs a church programme to get minor offenders out of prison. He organizes the money to pay fines or get bail for thousands of petty offenders who have to pay a fine of as little as US$25 but do not have the money, so go to prison instead. In 2001 lawyers working for the church reviewed the cases of half the prisoners in the city's three jails, 11,000 altogether. They found 4,000 were in prison because no money for bail or fines could be raised. All were released when the money was found.[47]

Father Cullen is also a priest, but a long way from Mexico. He has worked in Zambia for many years, and writes emails to his friends. One of these email messages described his daily work:

Last Wednesday I said Mass in one of the four prisons I go to …. I take a group from the parish, usually to do the singing…. They like to collect money to give the prisoners something. Last Wednesday each of the 250 prisoners got a little packet of salt and a piece of fairy soap, each bar being cut into five pieces. The prison authorities don't give out soap and often not salt to put into the dull, meagre one meal a day the men get, so the inmates were delighted with what they received. Scabies is a big problem and at times we take what is required to kill the lice and bed bugs.

Last Sunday I was in still another prison, the Central. There some 1,300 men at least are herded into a very small space, with no room to lie down at night because of the cramped conditions. After Mass again I had a list of needs…. There are 78 TB patients in the prison, and with the congestion, it surely gets passed on to others. Also there is a chronic outbreak of scabies, and about three-quarters of the prison population have rashes on their bodies.

Paul Heritage is an academic at London University. He is also a drama producer. In 1991 he started working in Brazil. Since then he has been running a programme, Staging Human Rights, in which he has worked with over 3,000 prisoners and prison staff across Brazil. Currently he is working with juveniles in the juvenile detention system of Rio de Janeiro, involving the young people in writing plays and acting. He tells of one visit to a juvenile detention centre.

One of my first visits to a Rio unit, I was taken round the installations. They were Dantesque…. The unit was built as a prison and operates as such. The young men were held in sub-human conditions not fit for any prisoner. At the end of the visit, I asked to see where young people were held if they committed an offence inside the prison. I was told that the cells had been de-activated. I asked to see them. I was taken to them, and there were 20 young people – most of them only in shorts and without footwear in a cellar without light and open sewage dripping in…. The boys were let out into the yard at my request. Their bodies were covered in cuts and bites – they were in a totally disgusting state.

I have never seen such appalling conditions during 15 years of working in prisons. I was visiting with the vice-director.... He was also shocked. I said that I would not leave until the boys were removed from that space. It was a very tense moment. The boys were moved.[48]

Mrs Chimaliro is a first grade magistrate in Malawi and a visiting justice of the peace. This means she has a duty to visit prisons to ensure that they are being run properly. Many judges and magistrates in different parts of the world have this duty, but not all take it as seriously as Mrs Chimaliro. She visits the prison in Mzuzu at any time without giving notice in advance to the police or the prison authorities because, she says, 'the police and prison have a tendency of cleaning their houses first before a visitor comes. As a result, when you come in, you may feel all is well.... I don't tolerate that.' She is not afraid of making her visits to the prison. 'It's true some magistrates fear visiting the prison. I don't see why ... we are mandated to do that: it's our job. I feel that if magistrates pass fair judgments there is no way he or she should fear visiting the prison.' She has strong views about prisoners' rights, especially on issues like 'right to a fair trial, right to bail, right to food, issues of sanitation'.

Her first task when visiting is to deal with the pre-trial prisoners who have not yet had a court appearance. She says:

I screen cases right there in prison ... as long as there is evidence sufficing release on bail, I do that. This makes the police to be alert at all times by not incarcerating people arbitrarily. A good example is a case involving a juvenile who was in prison for three months for allegedly stealing eight pieces of cassava. I didn't see any reason why he should have not been brought to court and I released him on bail.

Her second priority on her prison visits is to check the living conditions. She looks at the neatness of the cells and toilets, and checks the capacity of each cell. She compares the capacity of the cell with the number of suspects in the cell on that particular day and notes any outbreaks of disease. She also checks whether convicts have uniforms, whether remanded prisoners have blankets and whether juveniles are mixed with adults. She visits the kitchen and tastes the food. Sometimes her visit takes a whole day. Then she writes a report and sends it to all the authorities who need to know and should take action. Later, she checks if they have taken action. She does all this because she believes that prisoners should be treated properly and their rights respected.[49]

Many thousands of people like Mrs Chimaliro, whether they be *juges d'application des peines* in France, or members of Independent Monitoring Boards in England, carry out such work, often without recognition or much public interest.

Zachary Steel works as a psychiatrist in New South Wales in Australia. In 1992 he became concerned about the effects that detention was having on the mental health of refugees seeking asylum in Australia and locked up under harsh Australian immigration laws. It took ten years before he was able to gather enough material to depict the suffering inflicted on detained refugees. He started producing reports and papers about their experiences. Gradually Australians began to listen and a movement developed. Its supporters began to visit the detention centres and make friends with the people held there. Recently the numbers held have fallen and most of the children held in the centres have been released.[50]

Using the Law to Protect Prisoners

Much prison reform comes from successful court cases that establish the unlawfulness of a certain practice or require a government to make redress to prisoners who have been harmed, or to their dependants if loss of life is involved. Such cases are often brought by non-governmental organizations that specialize in using the law to protect and strengthen prisoners' rights. This is very much the practice of prison reform groups in the United States. In 2004 the American Civil Liberties Union filed a lawsuit on behalf of a gay African-American man who was repeatedly raped by Texas prison gangs. They wanted to establish that prison officials should have protected him.[51]

Some international organizations work with domestic groups to take cases through the national and international legal machinery. The Center for Justice and International Law (CEJIL) is based in Washington DC and has offices in San José, Costa Rica and Rio de Janeiro.[52] It specializes in taking cases through the inter-American system, defending them before the Inter-American Commission on Human Rights and the Inter-American Court of Human Rights. Interights, based in the United Kingdom, helps lawyers and others to prepare cases to be heard in national, regional and international courts.[53] The Aire Centre does similar work in Europe.[54]

Reducing the Use of Prison

In the United States, where the injustices are so glaring and the criminal justice system so harsh, change is being called for not just by outside reformers but by voices at the heart of the system. Justice Anthony Kennedy, a judge on the United States Supreme Court, said to the American Bar Association in 2003:

> In some cities, more than 50 per cent of young African-American men are under the supervision of the criminal justice system.... Our resources are misspent, our punishments too severe, our sentences too long.[55]

Following his speech, the American Bar Association set up a Commission chaired by Justice Kennedy. The Commission published a report proposing many basic reforms to the system in order to reduce the use of imprisonment and to emphasize rehabilitation rather than mere punishment.[56] More states in the US are now developing drug treatment instead of punishment. Organizations are looking at the effects of so much imprisonment on particular neighbourhoods and asking if they could not spend the money more fruitfully for the public good.

We have seen that improving prisons and respecting human rights has widespread support across the world. Reducing the use of prison is more difficult. Arguing the case against sending people to prison and suggesting alternatives is not easy. It takes courage for a politician to decide to try to reduce the number of prisoners. Yet there are many around the world who have decided to try and do it. Many others say that they want to do it but public opinion does not let them. In private they would agree: 'Yes we have too many prisoners.' In public, however, they would fear the stories in the newspapers: 'politician soft on crime', 'politician angers crime victims', 'politician wants to free murderers and robbers'. How far do these views reflect what people actually think?

In Chapter 2 some results from the International Crime Victim Survey about relative crime rates were reported. The survey also collects information on attitudes to punishment in various countries. It is carried out by asking interviewees what sentence they would like to see imposed on a person who committed a certain crime. The crime chosen was that of breaking into a house and stealing a colour television set. The burglar was a man aged 21 who had committed one burglary before. The survey covered 14 Western countries.

As Table 5.1 shows, one-third of all those who were asked their opinion said that the burglar should go to prison. Four out of ten said he should do work for the benefit of the community. Eleven per cent said he should pay a fine. However, these averages conceal big differences between countries. The country with the highest proportion of people in favour of a prison sentence for the burglar is the USA, with 56 per cent, followed by Japan and England and Wales, both at 51 per cent. At the bottom is Catalonia in Spain, where 7 per cent wanted prison, and France, where 12 per cent wanted prison. It would appear that generally English-speaking countries are more in favour of imprisoning people.[57]

Studies have also been carried out to ask the public what is the best way to spend money in order to reduce crime. Most surveys

Table 5.1
Sentence preference for a young recidivist burglar (percentages)

	Fine	Prison	Community service	Suspended sentence	Other sentence
USA	9	56	20	1	8
N Ireland	8	54	30	4	2
Scotland	11	52	24	5	4
Japan	17	51	19		1
England & Wales	7	51	28	5	4
Canada	9	45	32	4	7
Netherlands	11	37	30	10	5
Australia	8	36	46	3	3
Sweden	11	31	47	4	3
Portugal	9	26	54	1	6
Belgium	11	21	57	5	3
Poland	10	21	55	6	4
Denmark	9	20	50	13	4
Finland	15	19	46	16	2
France	8	12	69	5	2
Catalonia (Spain)	15	7	65	1	3
Average	11	34	41	6	4

Source: *Criminal Victimisation in Seventeen Industrialised Countries: Key Findings from the 2000 International Crime Victim Survey*, 2001.[58]

show that spending more money on prisons and punishment is not the most popular choice. Research carried out in South Africa in 2003 asked selected members of the public what would reduce crime in their areas. They were given a choice between more social development, more law enforcement or more and harsher punishment. Over half opted for more social development, under a quarter for more police and law enforcement and under a quarter for more punishments.[59]

Canada is a country where a political decision was taken to reduce the prison population. In the early 1990s the prison population was rising sharply. A decision was made that a continually rising prison population was not something Canada wanted to live with. The rise could be stopped by the implementation of alternative policies. So in 1995 the government introduced a new strategy. They brought together all the responsible actors in the provinces, federal government and territorial governments to agree a plan.[60] In 1996 a reform of sentencing was introduced and in particular a new sentence called 'the conditional sentence' was introduced. This is a prison sentence with a difference. The convicted person does not have to go to prison if he or she agrees to a range of conditions such as staying at home between certain hours and taking treatment for addiction.[61]

Why did this happen in Canada? Perhaps the policies of their nearest neighbour, the US, so shocked them that Canadians decided they had to try another way. Perhaps they decided there were better ways of spending Canadian public money than locking up so many people. In any case, it achieved its objectives. The imprisonment rate in Canada fell from 131 per 100,000 in 1994/5 to 116 per 100,000 in 2002.

In Finland, the prison population has stayed more or less stable for many years. Community work as a new punishment was introduced in 1994 as a means of keeping it stable. The law makers wanted to make sure that this new sentence was used to replace existing prison sentences, so it was introduced within a system that required the judge to decide first, 'This person will go to prison for a certain length of time.' Then, if the length of time was eight months or less, the sentence would be changed to community service unless there were very good arguments against it.[62]

In May 2004 the Federal Secretary of Public Security of Mexico, Dr Alejandro Gertz Manero, announced that the government was going to replace prison sentences by community work for low-value property crimes, which would lead to the release of 12,000 prisoners. In an interview Dr Gertz advised that failure to adopt the proposals would result in a need for 60 new prisons over the next six years. The plans were published for consultation by Mexico's state governments which have responsibility for most of the country's 449 prisons.[63]

The Canadian and Finnish stories and the plan from Mexico illustrate a substantial achievement. Introducing what are called 'alternatives to prison' is often seized on enthusiastically by reformers as an answer to overcrowded prisons and as the means to a more humane and socially inclusive punishment system. Unfortunately, it is not so simple. Introducing alternative sentences does not necessarily solve any criminal justice problems. It may just make the problems worse. Introducing alternatives to prison will be a reform measure only if the new sentences are really used instead of prison and are not just seized upon by judges as a good idea for punishing more people. If they are used for people who would not have gone to prison anyway, then the penal net is being widened and more fishes will be caught in it. This is why criminologists call this process 'net widening'. Even if the judges are convinced and would be happy to send a convicted person to do community work in the local area, they may fear the public reaction if someone convicted of a crime goes straight back into the neighbourhood rather than being locked up somewhere else.

If the judges and the public are to be convinced, then alternative sentences have to be seen as a serious option. The responsible authorities have to believe in them and want to sell them to the public by explaining why they are better than prison for many of the minor criminals languishing in prison, as well as for the public. They also have to convince judges that there is a workable system for managing alternative sentences. Offenders have to be supervised effectively. The community work has to be done. There has to be a guarantee that the convicted person cannot pay someone else to do the work, or pay the supervisor to record an attendance when there is no attendance. It is also important to decide with the judge which convicted people are eligible for non-prison punishments. It could be, for example, that all those sentenced to prison sentences of up to two years should be considered. Involving judges in the process so

Table 5.2
Possible alternative sentences

Fines	Money has to be paid to the state or sometimes as compensation to the victim or a contribution to a charitable fund.
Supervision	Can be done by a respected community member, social worker, probation officer or paralegal worker.
Community work (unpaid)	Needs to be supervised – convicted people can work in agriculture or improving the countryside, helping the sick and disabled, or making things for sale for good causes.
House arrest	Offenders' movements can be curtailed by requiring them to stay at home at certain times, or their movements can be monitored by electronic devices attached to the person to prevent them going to certain places.
Treatment	It can be a requirement that offenders attend a course of treatment for an addiction or other behaviour such as domestic violence.
Combination measures	The requirements listed above may be combined: for example, a fine and supervision.

that from time to time they see people doing community work or meet the satisfied beneficiaries – the users, say, of a garden built by convicted people – helps to win their confidence.

Reducing Pre-trial Detention

Not all the people in prison have been convicted. Many may spend months or even years locked up, just waiting for the case against them to be presented in court. Sometimes they stay in prison longer than they would have done if they had been convicted and sentenced.

This is a particular injustice since they have lost their liberty even though they have not been convicted. The case against them might not be proved and they will then be freed, but will still have spent time in prison, where they may have caught infectious diseases. By the time his innocence is established, an awaiting-trial prisoner may have lost his job, his home – if the rent was not paid while he was locked up – and also his good name.

In Malawi many people wait years for their case to come to trial. There are not enough lawyers to represent them and most of these accused cannot afford to pay a lawyer. But pre-trial prisoners in Malawi are now getting help. Edward Gama joined the Paralegal Advisory Service in Malawi in 2002. He goes to the prison regularly to run a paralegal clinic. He signs in there at 9 am, and is searched. Once inside the prison, it is time to meet the prisoners. 'They usually greet you before you have the time to greet them,' he says, 'as you will find them already gathered.' The prisoners are grouped according to the nature of the offence with which they are charged – homicide, for instance.

> We then arrange a seating plan, there are introductions to those who are new ... and 'icebreakers' to get everybody into the PLC (paralegal clinic) mood by playing games or singing songs. Then we introduce the topic of the day. *Belo eyah eeh, aah yee eya ee, Belo ndi ufulu wanga!* ('bail is my constitutional right') songs, adapted to a traditional tune, bring a point home and help prisoners to remember important elements (in a plea in mitigation and on bail, for instance) and it becomes fantastic as all the participants sing along even when taking a bath.

'Flip charts', he says, 'may be useful for educated fellows, but it honestly proved a flop for illiterate prisoners. So we turned to the use of drama and role plays, which make the sessions more exciting.' A drama is enacted that explains the difference between murder and manslaughter. A role play acts out the various defences to murder, such as having an alibi, self-defence, or insanity. After the group session, Edward Gama helps prisoners fill out the many forms that are needed for bail, appeals and other legal processes.[64]

In Bihar, India, on the last Saturday of every month, judicial officials visit the prisons and set up impromptu courts. The superintendent of the prison presents them with a list of those prisoners who have been waiting a long time for trial for non-serious offences or have been imprisoned for very minor infractions. The judicial officers deal with the cases on the spot. On one Saturday, about 5,383 petty criminal cases were disposed of in a single day.[65]

In the Philippines in 2004, a group of lawyers set up a national centre for legal aid to help poor people who could not afford a lawyer. They worked in the prisons in Quezon City and Pasig City, and the work led very quickly to the release of 42 prisoners. Some of these were clearly not guilty and others had spent a long time in prison because of delays in the system.[66]

So, reducing the number of people held in detention before their trial and getting out of prison people accused of minor crimes is an important activity and many prison reform activists are engaged in it.

A New View of Punishment

It is sometimes said that reforming prisons is not a path that real reformers should take. If prisons are reformed, it is argued, then they will become more acceptable. Judges will send more people to them and the public will see no need to become involved in improving them. That argument is not an easy one to accept. There will be prisons for the foreseeable future and they should not be places of torture, disease and inhumanity. But there is strength in the argument that prison reformers should not stop their efforts at the prison gate. As part of their reform they need continuously to ask the questions, 'Why are these people here? Should these people be locked up here? Why are all the people in this prison poor and powerless?' A good prison reform strategy always has in it a questioning strand and the hope that it will be possible to get some people out of prison.

Some reformers go further and use their energy to ask a more fundamental question. Can we find a vision of a different way? Archbishop Tutu asks this question in the extract at the beginning of this chapter. He talks of a process that looks for healing, a restoration of harmony. This new direction is much talked of around the world. Some call it restorative justice. Others have described it as 'transformative justice'. In practice this new approach to justice puts the emphasis on the relationship between the victim of the crime and the perpetrator. It looks for a solution that gives some satisfaction to the victims through processes such as apologizing, compensation or restitution. And it tries to bring the perpetrator to an understanding of the wrong that has been done.

These ideas are finding expression in criminal justice systems in various ways. In England and Wales young people found guilty of crime are involved in schemes of reparation and recompense to their victims. In New Zealand the process has gone much further and the whole system of dealing with young people who have been convicted of an offence is based on trying to work out some reconciliation through restitution. The New Zealand system is based on a 'conference' which brings together the young person, with his or her family and other supporters, and the victim, likewise in the company of supporters. The 'conference' is chaired by a government official from the Social Welfare Department who works to achieve an agreement between all the parties for a plan of restitution which satisfies the victim. This plan takes the place of any punishment imposed by a court.[67]

Versions of this restorative justice idea are also in place in Australia, Canada and the United States, and there is considerable activity on the international scene to promote the ideas and start new experiments with this very different form of justice.

A Return to Social Interventions

We have seen how far crime control in some countries has moved away from the local level, from communities and neighbourhoods. Brooklyn is a part of New York State, just across the bridge from Manhattan. It is a city of two and a half million people. In 2003 some of the people who live in Brooklyn discovered that they lived in 'million-dollar blocks'. A 'million-dollar block' is a small area of a few streets where at a least a million dollars is spent imprisoning people who live in these streets when not in prison. In Brooklyn in 2003 there were at least 35 such blocks.

This information can be gleaned only when the home addresses of the people sent to prison are entered on a map. Such a map shows that the people who go to prison come from very specific areas. Some areas produce no prisoners. Other areas produce many prisoners. Not surprisingly, the areas with the prisoners are the areas with high unemployment, low incomes, single-parent families, and poor housing.

An organization has been set up in New York, the Justice Mapping Center, which analyses where prisoners come from and adds up the costs. Then the question is asked, 'Is this the best way to spend a million dollars?' The local area gets no benefit from that money. On their return the men and women who have been sent to prison still need drug treatment, training for a job, mental health care, or basic education. All these services have to be provided locally. The million dollars spent on sending the residents of a poor neighbourhood to prison may buy the community some safety and peace and quiet if the people sent to prison are dangerous and violent. But many of those sent to prison are not dangerous or violent. The money spent on its residents gives nothing to the community where they live. No treatment centre is opened with it. No job-training programme is provided with it. None of it is invested, so none of it gives the neighbourhood any lasting benefit.

Dennis Maloney lives in Oregon, in the United States. He has worked in prisons all his working life. One of his functions as a prison warden was to sit on the State of Oregon committee that forecasts how many prison places will be needed in the years ahead. Dennis Maloney has five daughters. At one point he realized he was producing plans for places to lock up a proportion of the children in his daughter's kindergarten class in the prisons of the future. Suddenly he couldn't bear the thought, the idea that it was inevitable, that locking up people would just go on and on, and that the number of children destined for prison would go on growing.

So he resigned from the prison forecasting committee and got a new job where he could try something else. He started with young people who were sent to prison. He persuaded everyone in his county to do things a different way with these young people. If young people went to state prison, the money came from the state, not from his county. He persuaded the state to give back the money spent on imprisoning young people from his county. The county could do what they liked with the money, but if they sent a young person to the state prison they would have to pay for the place. The county decided to do things a different way and get a bit more for the money than seeing it disappear into the state prison budget so that they could lock up young people and send them back a bit worse.

So they set up projects involving a well-publicized community service delivering very visible benefits, supported by preventive and rehabilitative services. The judges were persuaded. Only a few very serious young offenders went to prison. Imprisonment was reduced by 74 per cent. The county got more services that benefited all young people. There was a lot of project work well done, a sense of ownership of the crime problem, and a more cohesive society.[68]

This idea, called 'Justice Reinvestment', shifts the power to make decisions about criminal justice from national to local level: it promotes local solutions to local problems and transfers budgets from ineffective crime control to more promising social expenditure and long-term investment in neighbourhoods.

What Is to Be Done?

First, prisons must be improved. There can be no argument for keeping people in the conditions endured by many of the world's prisoners. To do this, reformers must know what reform is and not expend their energy on making the unacceptable a little less painful. We heard how in Japan the leather restraining belt has been replaced by felt-lined handcuffs. Maybe these restrain less fatally, but changing a restraining belt for handcuffs is not enough. In England, Constance Lytton's fight to win the vote for women landed her in prison in London in 1909. She wondered why there was wire netting stretched right across the prison galleries – and discovered that it was to prevent the women throwing themselves from the upper floors to commit suicide. Better, she thought, to deal with their suicidal state than to unroll and fix wire netting.[69]

In Eastern Europe and Central Asia an epidemic of tuberculosis has swept through the prisons. Outside organizations have come in to help. They diagnose who is infected by analysis of their sputum. They have discovered, to their total disbelief, that infected sputum is traded and sold. Prisoners are prepared to risk becoming infected with TB in order to get out of the prison they are in and into a prison hospital where the treatment will be better and they will be properly fed. The response is not to condemn the prisoners but to start improving the whole system.

But all prison reformers face a dilemma, one well expressed by Angela Davies, once a prisoner herself and now a professor of the history of consciousness at the University of California, Santa Cruz:

> A major challenge of this movement is to do the work that will create more humane, habitable environments for people in prison without bolstering the permanence of the prison system.[70]

Unless they ask the right questions, prison reformers will not get beyond making small improvements that barely scratch the surface of what has to be done. What are the principles on which this place is run? How is power used? Is it abused? Why is there a shortage of food and medicine? Where is the food going? Humanitarian intervention is often essential, but it is not enough. Alternatives to prison should be developed but only within a context in which the important questions are being asked. Who is in prison? Should they be in prison? Are they so dangerous that public protection requires them to be locked up? Or are they just the small fry? Are they here because of the shortage of other services such as drug treatment or education? Prison reformers should also keep their minds on the need for prisoners to be protected by law, to have access to lawyers and redress for abuses. The idea of retribution should be challenged and other forms of holding people to account should be developed and nurtured.

Making change in this sector is an uphill task. There are many vested interests. Therefore, those supporting reform need to be strengthened by joining together and working together to develop a credible message. Places to look for support for reform include religious organizations and lawyers with an interest in human rights. Prison staff, because of their interest in improving their working conditions and safety, are often keen to support reform movements and sometimes take the lead. Organizations concerned for children can be encouraged to take up the cause of children and young people in prison. Women's organizations are often concerned about women in prison. Public health organizations can be involved through a concern about the spread of infectious diseases in prison.

Join the Reform Movement

This chapter has shown that governments, officials within the system, civil society groups and dedicated individuals are working all over the world to make prisons more civilized places and to look for better ways of dealing with those who are accused or convicted of breaking the criminal law. These groups do well, but the situation requires much more. Unless it takes a much wider view, the penal reform movement will not make much headway against pressure from marketization and the globalization of ideas about risk, risky people and the need to control them.

In Chapter 6 we look at the challenges now facing penal reformers and at a new agenda for integrating social justice and criminal justice.

Notes

1 Archbishop Desmond Tutu, *The Third Longford Lecture*, organized by the Frank Longford Charitable Trust working in association with the Prison Reform Trust, London, 16 February 2004.

2 See Marc Mauer, Ryan S. King and Malcolm C. Young, *The Meaning of 'Life': Long Prison Sentences in Context*, Washington DC: The Sentencing Project, May 2004.

3 Jon Henley, 'A Harsh Lesson for Les Misérables', *Guardian*, 8 August 2002.

4 William Omaria, 'Afterword', in *Prison Conditions in Africa: Report of a Pan-African Seminar, Kampala, Uganda 19–21 September 1996*, Paris: Penal Reform International, 1997, pp. 90–1.

5 US Department of Justice, *Capital Punishment 2003*, Washington DC: Bureau of Justice Statistics, 2004.

6 'Governor Clears Illinois Death Row', BBC News, 11 January 2003.

7 *Roper v. Simmons, No. 03-633,* argued 13 October 2004. On 1 March 2005 the US Supreme Court held that the Eighth and Fourteenth Amendments forbid the execution of offenders who were under the age of 18 when their crimes were committed.

8 Nelson Mandela, *Long Walk to Freedom*, London: Little, Brown and Company, 1994, p. 388.

9 University of KwaZulu–Natal, 'Performance Studies, Prison Theatre, 2004' on <www.ukzn.ac.za>.

10 In all, 102 states have ratified the Covenant and four – one of which is the United States – have signed but not ratified it.

11 International Covenant on Civil and Political Rights, Article 10.

12 International Covenant on Civil and Political Rights, Article 9.

13 International Covenant on Civil and Political Rights, Article 6.

14 International Covenant on Civil and Political Rights, Article 7 and UN Convention Against Torture and Other Cruel, Inhuman or Degrading Treatment or Punishment.

15 International Covenant on Civil and Political Rights, Article 14 (2).

16 International Covenant on Civil and Political Rights, Article 10 (3).

17 For example, UN Body of Principles for the Protection of All Persons under Any Form of Detention or Imprisonment, UN Standard Minimum Rules for the Treatment of Prisoners, UN Basic Principles for the Treatment of Prisoners, Convention on the Rights of the Child, European Convention on Human Rights, African Charter on Human and People's Rights, American Convention on Human Rights, European Prison Rules, and Principles of Medical Ethics relevant to the Role of Health Personnel, particularly Physicians, in the Protection of Prisoners and Detainees against Torture and Other Cruel, Inhuman or Degrading Treatment or Punishment.

18 '"Drunk Guards" Blamed for Prison Fire Deaths', Ananova press agency, 23 August 2001.

19 See International Centre for Prison Studies, 'Measuring and Evaluating Project Outcomes' in *Guidance Notes on Prison Reform*, 2004.

20 Association for the Prevention of Torture and Inter-American Institute of Human Rights, *Optional Protocol to the United Nations Convention against Torture and other Cruel, Inhuman or Degrading Treatment or Punishment: A Manual for Prevention*, San José and Geneva, 2004.

21 National Human Rights Commission of the Republic of Korea, *Report on Main Activities in 2002 and Plan in 2003*, Seoul, 2003, p. 13.

22 'Ejecutivo y Legislativo de Acuerdo en Declarar la Emergencia Carcelaria', *El Universal*, Venezuela, 14 October 2004.

23 Ministry of Justice of Venezuela, press releases, November 2004.

24 'Inmate Mothers to Keep Children', BBC News, 15 August 2004.

25 See Anne Applebaum, *Gulag: a History of the Soviet Camps*, London: Allen Lane, 2003, p. 67.

26 Personal communication from Kazakhstan.

27 Veronique Vasseur, *Médecin-Chef a la Prison de la Santé*, Paris: Le Cherche Midi Editeur, 2000, p. 34.

28 *Ibid.*, p. 37.

29 *Ibid.*, p. 30.

30 Andrew Coyle and Vivien Stern, 'Captive Populations: Prison Health Care', in Judith Healy and Martin McKee (eds), *Assessing Health Care: Responding to Diversity*, Oxford: Oxford University Press, 2004, pp. 116–17.

31 'Lithuania AIDS Prison: HIV Outbreak Hits Lithuanian Prisons', Agence France-Presse, 23 May 2002.

32 Ministry of the Interior and Ministry of Health, *Needle Exchange in Prison, Framework Document*, Spain, October 2002.

33 Center for Prisoners' Rights, *The Latest Situation of Japanese Prisons*, Japan, 2004, p. 2.

34 'Group Slams Solitary Confinement', *Herald Tribune Asahi*, 12 February 2002.

35 See, for example, UN Economic and Social Council, Administration of Justice, *Written Statement Submitted by Japan Fellowship of Reconciliation*, 22 July 2002.

36 'Anal Torture Death Brings Indictment', *Japan Times*, 5 March 2003.

37 Takuya Asakura, 'Prison Abuses in Spotlight Following Guard Arrests', *Japan Times*, 12 November 2002.

38 'Moriyama Vows to Examine Prisoners' Complaints', *Japan Times*, 22 February 2003.

39 Hiroshi Matsubara, 'New Correctional Reform Panel Launched', *Japan Times*, 1 April 2003.

40 Hiroshi Matsubara, 'Ministry to Replace Dreaded Prison Device', *Japan Times*, 18 June 2003.

41 Hiroshi Matsubara, 'Ministry Vows Immediate Steps to Improve Correctional System', *Japan Times*, 23 December 2003.

42 Penal Reform International, newsletter No. 51, December 2002, p. 5.

43 *InfoChange News and Features*, March 2004.

44 See <www.genepi.fr>.

45 'Human Rights Defenders in Iran Continue to Suffer Harassment', *The Wire* (Amnesty International magazine), September 2004.

46 See <www.justiceaction.org.au>.

47 Kevin Sullivan and Mary Jordan, 'Disparate Justice Imprisons Mexico's Poor', *Washington Post*, 6 July 2002.

48 Mayra Jucá, 'NGO Takes Theatre into Brazilian Prisons and Juvenile Detention Centres', Children and Youth in Organised Armed Violence, <www.coav.org.br>.

49 Paralegal Advisory Service, *Newsletter 5*, August 2004, p. 2.

50 Caroline Moorehead, *Human Cargo*, London: Chatto and Windus, 2005, pp. 118–21.

51 'ACLU Hails Important Step Forward in Shocking Prison Sex Slave Case', 9 September 2004, <www.aclu.org.>.

52 See <www.cejil.org>.

53 See <www.interights.org>.

54 See <www.airecentre.org>.

55 *Speech at the American Bar Association Annual Meeting* by Anthony M. Kennedy, Associate Justice, Supreme Court of the United States, 9 August 2003.

56 American Bar Association, *Justice Kennedy Commission, Reports with Recommendations to the ABA House of Delegates,* August 2004.

57 See John van Kesteren, Pat Mayhew and Paul Mieuwbeerta, *Criminal Victimisation in Seventeen Industrialised Countries: Key Findings from the 2000 International Crime Victim Survey,* The Hague: Wetenschappelijk Onderzoeks-en Documentatiecentrum (WODC), 2001, p. 87.

58 *Ibid.*

59 Institute for Security Studies, South Africa, 2003.

60 Solicitor-General of Canada, *Corrections Population Growth Second Progress Report for the Federal/ Provincial/Territorial Ministers for Justice,* Regina, Saskatchewan, 1998, p. 1.

61 Bill C-41 (1996), Canadian Criminal Code.

62 Tapio Lappi-Seppälä, 'Regulating the Prison Population, Experiences from a Long Term Policy in Finland', paper delivered to the International Symposium of the European Permanent Conference on Probation (CEP) on 'Probation: a European Perspective', Malta, 29 March 2001.

63 Adapted from press reports of interviews with Dr Gertz, 2004.

64 Paralegal Advisory Service, *Newsletter 5,* Malawi, August 2004, pp. 3–4.

65 Penal Reform International, *Good Practices in Reducing Pre-Trial Detention,* London, 2003.

66 'New Judicial Reforms in Philippines Aim to Address Needs of Poor', *Choices* (United Nations Development Programme magazine), March 2004.

67 Vivien Stern, *A Sin Against the Future: Imprisonment in the World,* Boston, Northeastern University Press, 1998, pp. 323–32.

68 'Justice Reinvestment', *Ideas for an Open Society,* 3, 3 (November 2003), Open Society Institute, New York.

69 Constance Lytton, *Prisons and Prisoners,* London: Virago, 1988, p. 178.

70 Angela Y. Davis, *Are Prisons Obsolete?,* New York: Seven Stories Press, 2003, p. 103.

6

Criminal Justice and Social Justice

In many countries, social justice has been reduced to criminal justice.

Eduardo Galeano 1998[1]

The Penal Journey

This book began in the burnt-out shell of Glendairy prison in Barbados, the scene of a prison riot that saw the prisoners shipped out and housed in disused warehouses. The question was asked, should the prison be kept as a museum or a historic site? This is unlikely. Although there is a prison in Brazil converted into an arts centre and one in Scotland turned into a very realistic nineteenth-century prison experience for tourists, few prisons have become museums or been converted to other functions. On the contrary, we have seen how the use of prison is booming. Most countries are increasing their prison places, stuffing more prisoners into over-populated cells, and looking to entrepreneurs to provide new prisons quickly on a 'buy now, pay later' basis.

Who are held in these dangerous and damaging places? In every one there is a minority for whom imprisonment can easily be justified, people who have committed terrible deeds or transgressed so far from society's norms in their actions that their place has to be behind locked doors. But, as we have seen, locking up such people is not the main work of prisons anymore. Prisons are being used in most countries to sweep up the unwanted, mainly urban, poor, the resented minorities, the sick for whom medical care is deemed too expensive, the uneducated for whom proper education is not deemed worthwhile, the unemployed for whom work is not available.

This book has taken the reader on a journey through some unpleasant places, to see things that are often hidden from the public view. We have been into the cells of dying prisoners and into courtrooms where prisoners are making claims about abuse and rape. We have learned of prisoners who are so mentally ill that they cover their bodies with their own faeces, and of the regular anal searches of prisoners even though they have not left their cells. We have discovered that new symbol of the inequity at the heart of the relationship between the rich and the poor world, the see-through lavatories in the airports of Europe. These lavatories aim to prevent poor people getting any financial benefit from risking their lives swallowing containers of an illegal product that consumers in rich countries want, and are prepared to pay for. We have discovered the countries that put damaged and fearful children in immigrant custody centres. We have learned the name of one of the many disturbed and badly behaved teenagers from the poor areas in England, whose names and pictures are publicised throughout their towns.

Fortunately, many people find these situations unacceptable and we have also encountered the army of reformers, the individuals who fight for prisoners' rights, get them released from prison, bring them the basics of life and expose abuses. We have met those within the system who improve what they can and wish they could do more.

Criminal Justice as It Should Be

We have also been given glimpses of what a criminal justice system that had justice at its heart might look like. Criminal justice has become so deformed by its misuse that its basic shape is now hard to discern. So it is important to assert that there must be a proper criminal justice system in every country that upholds the rule of law and maintains society's values. Decent criminal justice policies would be based on five principles.

The first is that *criminal justice has a small role to play in securing peace, security and public protection*. Criminalization and punishment should not extend into areas of health, relations in neighbourhoods, management of small-scale conflicts, control of migration. Social problems should receive social solutions. New crimes should rarely be created and old crimes should be considered for decriminalization. Children should be kept out of the criminal justice system.

Second, *the proper role of the criminal justice system is to deal with serious crime and to take it seriously*. In the case of the most serious crimes – murders, manslaughters, rapes and other acts of horrible violence – justice must be done and people must be protected. The values of society must be upheld. The reader of this book has met perpetrators of such serious crimes. Ronald Herrera, for instance, who was left to bleed to death in a Californian prison, was convicted of rape. Vyacheslav, who was held in the terrible conditions of Petak prison in Russia, had stabbed two women to death. Van der Ven, who was held in the high security unit in the Netherlands, was convicted of a number of violent offences.

In these cases, the criminal justice system is a moral expression of what societies believe in. 'Impunity' is unacceptable. Impunity is not a word criminal justice people use very much. It is usually heard in the context of human rights abusers: it is held to be imperative that they should not enjoy impunity, but should be held accountable for their crimes. This is what the attempt to bring General Pinochet to trial in Spain was about in the late 1990s. That is why the international community has established the International Criminal Court – where perpetrators of crimes against humanity and human rights abuses can be brought to justice – and why many countries in the world have ratified it, although not (as yet) the

United States. In these cases a proper and fair trial with public access, the passing of sentence and the imposition of a sanction all signal a recognition of the wrong done through a proper legitimate process. This process stamps the label of great wrong on the crime that was committed and rightness is again vindicated.

It does not follow at all that the consequence of such a finding by a tribunal has to be retributive punishment – great suffering imposed on the wrongdoer in order that the victims can feel avenged. The South African Truth and Reconciliation Commission has shown another way. Once the perpetrator has accepted responsibility and admitted guilt, forgiveness is a possible response.

A proper criminal justice system should also pay much more attention to the care of the victims of serious crime. A lesson can be taken from the way human rights violations and the victims of these crimes are treated. Serious crimes are not normally seen as human rights violations. Yet there is a parallel between victims of human rights violations and victims of serious crimes. They both suffer serious personal trauma. Victims of serious crimes and their relatives should be entitled to the sort of help, support and counselling that is given to victims of gross human rights abuses.

Third, there is the other sort of crime, the vast area of non-dangerous and not-so-serious crime that takes place in neighbourhoods and poor areas, and where the potential for more criminalization is virtually infinite. Here, *harm reduction is the key. Problem solving is the preferred option*. The aim should be to solve the conflict, satisfy the injured party and try not to damage the life chances of the perpetrator. Mediation and alternative dispute resolution are better options. The use of a harsh punishment such as imprisonment should be very rare when dealing with such cases, and other sanctions such as community service should be used. Many people mentioned in this book are candidates for this approach: for example, the five prisoners who were killed in Meru prison in Kenya, all locked up there for the most minor acts. Nikhat, in prison for five months in India for drug peddling, is a candidate, as is the American woman who was serving four years for a drug offence and was raped by a prison guard.

Fourth, there needs to be *a major shift in policy, towards providing safety for people without invoking the damaging label of crime, and without involving courts and punishment.* Here we need to see governments giving a much higher priority to the measures that make a neighbourhood safe and provide people with a sense of security. Money should be spent not on razor wire and closed circuit TV cameras but on creating social cohesion and providing the social goods that keep people from preying on each other, what the economist Amartya Sen calls 'effective institutions for the maintenance of local peace and order'.[2] The aim should be to turn negative and controlling mechanisms into positive, investing ones. Every time it is proposed to expand the law by creating a new crime, there should be detailed and lengthy scrutiny. The question 'Why is this necessary?' should always be asked. Can we achieve the objective another way? Every time another prison is proposed, there should be detailed analysis of what else the money could have been spent on, and what could be done with it to help those suffering most from crime and violence. Moves to control young people should be turned into moves to educate and involve young people. Policing should be suffused with ideas of turning confrontation into violence reduction. Every time a judge says of the defendant before him, 'This person needs help, not punishment,' the help should be available.

Finally, *the market in crime control must be discouraged.* The buying and selling of imprisonment is likely to result in pressure for its increased use, and therefore should be opposed. The market in crime control leads to a criminal justice system that emphasizes technological control at the expense of measures to promote social cohesion.

Why Should We Care about Prisoners and Prisons?

The five principles set out above are not just an agenda that should interest penal reformers. They also propose a debate that should concern a much wider constituency. This book has hoped to convince those who care about the way the world is going – the destruction of the environment, the growing gap between rich and poor, the diminishing interest in rights and the spread of repression in the name of a 'war on terror' – that they should also care about the growing number of prisoners in the world. They should care about the redefinition of many acts as crimes. They should see good reason to argue against the shift in spending from schools, health care and neighbourhood safety to punishment and prisons. They should be concerned about the failure to devise effective solutions to the violence and crime that surround poor people in their daily lives. They should look into the impact of the 'drug war' on the economies and social development of poor countries. They should be aware of the influences which lead poverty-stricken people into the immigration detention and removal centres of the rich West.

Perhaps, some may say, the time is not right for a new approach to dealing with crime and violence. A call for more concern about prisons and criminal justice will evoke little response. For many people, violence is becoming more of a reality and a restriction on their freedom to live their lives without fear. In the little Caribbean island of St Vincent, with a population of less than 120,000, there were 28 murders in 2004, the highest number ever in one year.[3] On a summer weekend in June 2005, families enjoying the sun on a Portuguese beach near Lisbon were alarmed when a group of 500 teenagers swept the beach *en masse*, robbing the sunbathers as they went.[4] How can anyone be moved by an argument that advocates opening the prison gates, releasing many of those held within, reducing the number of crimes, looking for a different way?

Let us try and answer that question.

We begin with effectiveness. Many commentators now talk about 'human security'. People are much less secure in many ways. Their livelihoods are fragile. Access to food and water are not assured. They may well become victims of attacks on themselves or their property. Does the move to greater prison populations, more crimes and harsher punishments lead to more human security and a reduction in violence? If so, it would be hard to argue against it.

The answer is no. The world is falling for the big lie that prison works and more criminalization works. In fact what actually reduces crime and violence are social measures to reduce crime and violence. From better street lighting to gun control, to activities for inner city adolescents, the experience of how to deal with crime and violence is widespread and the knowledge is available. In many places it is being put into practice.

In promoting the illusion that punishment and spreading the crime net wider are the answer, great injustices are being perpetrated. The poor are paying the price and neither the poor nor the rich are being well protected. The criminal justice system is no longer being used as a justice system in the sense understood in earlier decades. It is becoming an injustice system. On any one day, one out of every 14 children in the United States has a parent in prison. If imprisonment in the US continues at the same level, one out of every three black boys born in 2005 can expect to spend some time in prison.[5] People are being wasted. Huge resources are being spent on preventing human beings realizing their potential. The damage inflicted on certain families and the communities from which they come goes deep, and without remedial action its effects will last for generations. The imprisonment of large numbers of young men from certain neighbourhoods further destroys the capacity of those neighbourhoods to exert social control and instil pro-social values.

These ideas are spreading. In the space of 30 years the Netherlands has moved from running a justice system where prison was barely used (an imprisonment rate of 17 per 100,000) and every prisoner had a single cell and a full day's activity, to an imprisonment rate in 2005 of 123 per 100,000, prisoners sharing cells and limited activities. Japan in 1975 had 46,000 prisoners. In 1992 it had fewer, 45,000. In 2004 the figure was nearly 74,000. The United

States has an increase in its prison population every year. It seemed that when it reached two million it might start to go down. But latest figures show another increase, of nearly 50,000 prisoners. New South Wales in Australia has just announced it is building prison places for another 100 people. Soon this trend will spread to countries of the South and become part of the message of the aid donors: 'Imprisonment is good. Have more of it. Here's the money … as long as it's spent on private prisons.'

A Regional Approach

These trends are not the same in all parts of the world. We can distinguish four distinct strands. In the rich Western countries the criminal justice systems are succumbing, some more and some less, to the influence of the United States model of mass incarceration as a response to urban problems, criminalization of more acts and methods of creating deep exclusion of those deemed to be threats.

In Latin America and the Caribbean the system has been moulded by the security concerns of the great power of the region, the emphasis on combating drug trafficking and the export of gang members from the prisons of the United States to the lands of their birth, even if they left them as small children. The huge economic inequalities of this region add another ingredient to this boiling soup. These problems overwhelm the justice systems of Latin America, which are characterized by high prison populations and much violence in prisons.

In the poorest countries of the world, particularly in Africa, the imposition of ex-colonial resource-hungry criminal justice systems has led to near collapse in many countries, deep corruption and prison systems where many die. In some countries the justice system cannot rightly be called a justice system at all.

Former Soviet Union countries are still in the process of reforming systems which represented the apogee of repression and in these countries prison populations are being reduced and new approaches introduced. Whether this movement for reform can withstand the pressures from the 'war on terror' and the lack of interest in reform from the Western countries remains to be seen.

A Plan of Action

Much good can come from strong prison reform activities, but this is not enough. All those who want a more just world must find and develop the arguments against the growth of the criminal justice system, the increase in the number of acts defined as crimes, the inequality of their application, and the diversion of funds from positive social goods to negative and unproductive containment. This campaign will need dissemination of ideas and the development of explanations that make sense to people frightened of crime and suffering its consequences. These explanations must make it clear why the policies now spreading around the world will not make anyone safer.

The reform strategy must move to seek support from social activists in other fields. Social justice is imperilled as the criminal justice juggernaut moves deeper into social life. Education suffers as the money goes into prisons. Health care suffers as the money goes into prisons. Communities suffer as their young men are sent away and then return, angry and unemployable. The big task is to begin the shift back from prison spending to social spending, from criminal solutions to social solutions.

Criminalizing interventions rather than social interventions have taken over policy making and infiltrated the conversation, the language and the framework of social policy. To counteract these tendencies a rethink is needed and a search for an alternative approach that will make sense to those who work in the system, those who live in fear of crime from day to day and those whose behaviour needs to be curbed and changed. This new approach must try to counteract the centralizing forces and look much more to the local level and the local solution. A new strategy must emerge, located in the areas where crime is most frequent and from where the prisons are filled. These are the neighbourhoods where there is no investment until the time comes to send a resident off to prison. Then the investment starts but none of it benefits the neighbourhood or better fits the prisoner to live there on return. Campaigns are needed, not against criminals, but against crime. Vigilantes are needed, not to make the streets safer but to make the criminal justice system more just and to campaign for more local decision making. These decisions need to focus on the balance of crime policies in neighbourhoods, diverting expenditure towards youth, families, job training and new sanctions that make sense to the public, have some meaning for crime victims, and reduce harm to the benefit of all parties.

In those countries that receive foreign aid a strategy towards the donors should be developed. When donors in rich countries offer to build new prisons the recipient country should ask instead for the money to be given for gang rehabilitation projects, neighbourhood mediation centres, health and education. If rich countries are installing computers in the prison system to keep records of all the prisoners, the recipient country should ask for some for the gang rehabilitation projects too. If the donor is training judges, the recipient country should try and influence the training so that the judges learn about poverty, prevention and alternative sentencing. If donors give money for the establishment of a Western-style probation service, the recipient country could ask for the money to be redeployed to the training of paralegal workers and mediators from local communities.

Reformers must also reject most of what is being offered by the market, such as the big computer systems that store data about all the risky people, the electronic bracelets that stigmatize their wearers and give them nothing to improve their lives, the eyes in the sky that can track movements, the voice recognition systems and the biometric imaging.

The Future

If these changes are not set in place then there are great dangers. Who will be criminalized next – the environmental protester, perhaps, or the pacifist? Where will all this technological development lead? If convicted people can be electronically tagged, so can schoolchildren or workers. If lie detectors can be used with those convicted of sexual offences, perhaps they can be used in non-criminal settings too. If convicted people can be tracked by satellite, so can the whole population of the areas where 'risky' people live.

A criminal justice system in an environment of gross social injustice becomes a deformity. When a justice system becomes so unjust and a system for security makes us so insecure, it is time for a change.

Notes

1 Eduardo Galeano, *Upside Down,* New York: Picador, 1998, p. 30.
2 Quoted in Paul Farmer, *Pathologies of Power: Health, Human Rights and the New War on the Poor,* Berkeley: University of California Press, 2005.
3 Kenton Chance, 'St Vincent and Grenadines Minister Calls on Police to Be More Confidential', Caribbean News Net, 26 January 2005.
4 'Portugal Youths in Beach Rampage', BBC News, 11 June 2005.
5 Marc Mauer, 'Thinking about Prison and Its Impact in the Twenty-first Century', *Ohio State Journal of Criminal Law*, 2005, p. 612 .

Selected Further Reading

No reading list can cover this huge subject. The selection below gives the reader new to criminal justice a taste of ideas, history, different traditions and some contemporary realities.

Nils Christie, *Crime Control as Industry: Towards Gulags, Western-Style*, London: Routledge, 2nd edition, 1994.

Nils Christie, *A Suitable Amount of Crime*, London and New York: Routledge, 2004.

Andrew Coyle, *The Prisons We Deserve*, London: Harper Collins, 1994.

Andrew Coyle, Allison Campbell and Rodney Neufeld (eds), *Capitalist Punishment: Prison Privatization and Human Rights*, Atlanta and London: Clarity Press and Zed Books, 2003.

Amanda Dissel and Jody Kollapen, *Racism and Discrimination in the South African Penal System*, Centre for the Study of Violence and Reconciliation, Penal Reform International, 2002.

Paul Farmer, *Pathologies of Power: Health, Human Rights and the New War on the Poor*, Berkeley: University of California Press, 2005.

Eduardo Galeano, *Upside Down*, New York: Picador, 1998 (English edition 2000).

David Garland, *The Culture of Control: Crime and Social Order in Contemporary Society*, Oxford: Oxford University Press, 2001.

Ryszard Kapúsciński, *Imperium*, London: Granta Books, 1994.

Axel Klein, Marcus Day and Anthony Harriott (eds) *Caribbean Drugs: from Criminalization to Harm Reduction*, Kingston: Ian Randle, and London and New York: Zed Books, 2004.

Caroline Moorehead, *Human Cargo*, London: Chatto and Windus, 2005.

Rani D. Shankardass and Saraswati Haider, *Barred from Life, Scarred for Life: Experiences of Women in the Criminal Justice System*, Gurgaon: Penal Reform and Justice Association (PRAJA), 2004.

Harry Wu, *Bitter Winds*, New York: John Wiley and Sons, 1994.

Useful Websites

Amnesty International	www.amnesty.org
Drug Policy Alliance	www.drugpolicy.org
Human Rights Watch	www.hrw.org
International Centre for Prison Studies	www.prisonstudies.org
Penal Reform International	www.penalreform.org
Prison Privatisation International	www.psiru.org
Statewatch	www.statewatch.org

Index

Global Issues in a Changing World

This new series of short, accessible think-pieces deals with leading global issues of relevance to humanity today. Intended for the enquiring reader and social activists in the North and the South, as well as students, the books explain what is at stake and question conventional ideas and policies. Drawn from many different parts of the world, the series' authors pay particular attention to the needs and interests of ordinary people, whether living in the rich industrial or the developing countries. They all share a common objective – to help stimulate new thinking and social action in the opening years of the new century.

Global Issues in a Changing World is a joint initiative by Zed Books in collaboration with a number of partner publishers and nongovernmental organizations around the world. By working together, we intend to maximize the relevance and availability of the books published in the series.

Participating NGOs

Both ENDS, Amsterdam
Catholic Institute for International Relations, London
Corner House, Sturminster Newton
Council on International and Public Affairs, New York
Dag Hammarskjöld Foundation, Uppsala
Development GAP, Washington DC
Focus on the Global South, Bangkok
IBON, Manila
Inter Pares, Ottawa
Public Interest Research Centre, Delhi
Third World Network, Penang
Third World Network-Africa, Accra
World Development Movement, London

About this series

'Communities in the South are facing great difficulties in coping with global trends. I hope this brave new series will throw much needed light on the issues ahead and help us choose the right options.'
MARTIN KHOR, *Director,*
Third World Network, Penang

'There is no more important campaign than our struggle to bring the global economy under democratic control. But the issues are fearsomely complex. This Global Issues series is a valuable resource for the committed campaigner and the educated citizen.'
BARRY COATES, *Director,*
World Development Movement (WDM)

'Zed Books has long provided an inspiring list about the issues that touch and change people's lives. The Global Issues series is another dimension of Zed's fine record, allowing access to a range of subjects and authors that, to my knowledge, very few publishers have tried. I strongly recommend these new, powerful titles and this exciting series.'
JOHN PILGER, *author*

'We are all part of a generation that actually has the means to eliminate extreme poverty world-wide. Our task is to harness the forces of globalization for the benefit of working people, their families and their communities – that is our collective duty. The Global Issues series makes a powerful contribution to the global campaign for justice, sustainable and equitable development, and peaceful progress.'
GLENYS KINNOCK, *MEP*

The Global Issues series

For full details of this list and Zed's other subject and general catalogues, please write to: The Marketing Department, Zed Books, 7 Cynthia Street, London N1 9JF, UK or email Sales@zedbooks.net

Visit our website at: www.zedbooks.co.uk

Participating organizations

Both ENDS A service and advocacy organization which collaborates with environment and indigenous organizations, both in the South and in the North, with the aim of helping to create and sustain a vigilant and effective environmental movement.

Nieuwe Keizersgracht 45, 1018 vc Amsterdam, The Netherlands
Phone: +31 20 623 0823 • Fax: +31 20 620 8049
Email: info@bothends.org • Website: www.bothends.org

Catholic Institute for International Relations (CIIR) CIIR aims to contribute to the eradication of poverty through a programme that combines advocacy at national and international level with community-based development.

Unit 3, Canonbury Yard, 190a New North Road, London N1 7BJ, UK
Phone: +44 (0)20 7354 0883 • Fax +44 (0)20 7359 0017
Email: ciir@ciir.org • Website: www.ciir.org

Corner House The Corner House is a UK-based research and solidarity group working on social and environmental justice issues in North and South.

PO Box 3137, Station Road, Sturminster Newton, Dorset DT10 1YJ, UK
Tel.: +44 (0)1258 473795 • Fax: +44 (0)1258 473748
Email: cornerhouse@gn.apc.org • Website: www.cornerhouse.icaap.org

Council on International and Public Affairs (CIPA) CIPA is a human rights research, education and advocacy group, with a particular focus on economic and social rights in the USA and elsewhere around the world. Emphasis in recent years has been given to resistance to corporate domination.

777 United Nations Plaza, Suite 3C, NewYork, NY 10017, USA
Tel.: +1 212 972 9877 • Fax +1 212 972 9878
Email: cipany@igc.org • Website: www.cipa-apex.org

Dag Hammarskjöld Foundation The Dag Hammarskjöld Foundation, established in 1962, organizes seminars and workshops on social, economic and cultural issues facing developing countries with a particular focus on alternative and innovative solutions. Results are published in its journal *Development Dialogue*.

Övre Slottsgatan 2, 753 10 Uppsala, Sweden.
Tel.: +46 18 102772 • Fax: +46 18 122072
Email: secretariat@dhf.uu.se • Website: www.dhf.uu.se

Development GAP The Development Group for Alternative Policies is a Non-Profit Development Resource Organization working with popular organizations in the South and their Northern partners in support of a development that is truly sustainable and that advances social justice.

927 15th Street NW, 4th Floor, Washington, DC, 20005, USA
Tel.: +1 202 898 1566 • Fax: +1 202 898 1612
Email: dgap@igc.org • Website: www.developmentgap.org

Focus on the Global South Focus is dedicated to regional and global policy analysis and advocacy work. It works to strengthen the capacity of organizations of the poor and marginalized people of the South and to better analyse and understand the impacts of the globalization process on their daily lives.

C/o CUSPLI, Chulalongkorn University, Bangkok 10330, Thailand
Tel.: +66 2 218 7363 • Fax: +66 2 255 9976
Email: Admin@focusweb.org • Website: www.focusweb.org

IBON IBON Foundation is a research, education and information institution that provides publications and services on socio-economic issues as support to advocacy in the Philippines and abroad. Through its research and databank, formal and non-formal education programmes, media work and international networking, IBON aims to build the capacity of both Philippine and international organizations.

Room 303 SCC Bldg, 4427 Int. Old Sta. Mesa, Manila 1008, Philippines
Phone: +632 7132729 • Fax +632 716108
Email: editors@ibon.org • Website: www.ibon.org

Inter Pares Inter Pares, a Canadian social justice organization, has been active since 1975 in building relationships with Third World development groups and providing support for community-based development programmes. Inter Pares is also involved in education and advocacy in Canada, promoting understanding about the causes, effects and solutions to poverty.

221 Laurier Avenue East, Ottawa, Ontario, KIN 6PI Canada
Phone: +1 613 563 4801 • Fax +1 613 594 4704
Email: info@interpares.ca • Website: www.interpares.ca

Public Interest Research Centre PIRC is a research and campaigning group based in Delhi which seeks to serve the information needs of activists and organizations working on macro-economic issues concerning finance, trade and development.

142 Maitri Apartments, Plot No. 28, Patparganj, Delhi 110092, India Phone: +91 11 222I0SI/2432054 • Fax: +91 11 2224233
Email: kaval@nde.vsnl.net.in

Third World Network TWN is an international network of groups and individuals involved in efforts to bring about a greater articulation of the needs and rights of peoples in the Third World; a fair distribution of the world's resources; and forms of development which are ecologically sustainable and fulfil human needs. Its international secretariat is based in Penang, Malaysia.

121-S Jalan Utama, 10450 Penang, Malaysia
Tel.: +60 4 226 6159 • Fax: +60 4 226 4505
Email: twnet@po.jaring.my • Website: www.twnside.org.sg

Third World Network–Africa TWN–Africa is engaged in research and advocacy on economic, environmental and gender issues. In relation to its current particular interest in globalization and Africa, its work focuses on trade and investment, the extractive sectors and gender and economic reform.

2 Ollenu Street, East Legon, PO Box AN19452, Accra-North, Ghana. Tel.: +233 21 511189/503669/500419 • Fax: +233 21 511188
Email: twnafrica@ghana.com

World Development Movement (WDM) The World Development Movement campaigns to tackle the causes of poverty and injustice. It is a democratic membership movement that works with partners in the South to cancel unpayable debt and break the ties of IMF conditionality, for fairer trade and investment rules, and for strong international rules on multinationals.

25 Beehive Place, London SW9 7QR, UK
Tel.: +44 (0)20 7737 6215 • Fax: +44 (0)20 7274 8232
Email: wdm@wdm.org.uk • Website: www.wdm.org.uk